The Santa

LETTERS

The Santa LETTERS

STACY GOOCH-ANDERSON

Sweetwater Books
An imprint of Cedar Fort, Inc.
Springville, Utah

ISBN 13: 978-1-4621-1082-7

Published by Sweetwater Books, an imprint of Cedar Fort, Inc., 2373 W. 700 S., Springville, UT, 84663
Distributed by Cedar Fort, Inc., www.cedarfort.com

LIBRARY OF CONGRESS CATALOGING-IN-PUBLICATION DATA

Gooch-Anderson, Stacy, author.
 The Santa letters : a Christmas story / Stacy Gooch-Anderson.
   pages cm
 ISBN 978-1-4621-1082-7
1. Widows--Fiction. 2. Family counselors--Fiction. 3. Bereavement--Fiction. 4. Grief--Fiction.
5. Families--Fiction. 6. Christmas stories. I. Title.
 PS3601.N5474S26 2012
 813'.6--dc23
                    2012025829

Cover design by Angela D. Olsen
Cover design © 2012 by Lyle Mortimer
Edited and typeset by Lyndsee Simpson Cordes

Printed in the United States of America

10 9 8 7 6 5 4 3 2

Printed on acid-free paper

To my parents, William (Bill) and Laurel (Emma) Gooch; my sweetheart, Brad; and four sons, Justin, Mitch, Josh, and Maison; because they fill my life with the blessings of Christmas each and every day.

ACKNOWLEDGMENTS

I would be severely remiss if I did not first acknowledge a Savior whose sacrifice will one day allow me the opportunity to be reunited with those I have loved and lost and whose example has been as a beacon light of hope.

I must also acknowledge my family; my parents, Bill and Laurel, who gave me a strong foundation to build my life upon and fortified me when I began to crumble. It is then that they lifted me up and pushed me to greater heights.

And my brothers, Rex, David, Tim, and Taylor; my younger sister, Becky; and all of their spouses, Josh, Sydne, Shiloh, and Jennifer; and my in-laws, Janice and Lamont. They have listened to countless ramblings and given me valuable feedback and fertile ground to dream.

And thank you to the man who completes me and to our four sons, since they are the ones who've put up with my sleepless nights, editing binges, and tirades through writer's block and deadlines. But mostly because they have given me much of the characterization for anything I write and still love me even though I've made their lives an open book, so to speak.

ACKNOWLEDGMENTS

My sincere thanks also goes to Ruth Schmidt for her assistance in helping me with the legal standings and current national laws on cell phone usage while driving.

And lastly, I owe a debt of gratitude to my first editors, Linda Petersen and Sallie Young, who were patient and persistent as I honed my skills. And to Lyndsee Cordes, my current editor, and Kammi Rencher, who took a chance on me, and Lyle Mortimer and all of the other talented people at Sweetwater Books, for their help in bringing this special story to a new generation of Christmas-story lovers.

William raced back through the wooded trail as his three sons nipped at his heels. He had barely collapsed onto the patchwork quilt spread on the grass when he was accosted as his sons dog-piled on him, laughing that their dear old dad's days of keeping the lead were nearly at an end.

Emma casually brought up the rear, holding two-year-old McKenna's hands as she swung her from point to point. The last swing landed her on top of the pile, where she giggled at having conquered the heap.

Emma laughed as she watched thirteen-year-old Jesse pin his father with the help of nine-year-old Michael and eight-year-old Jaden. "You better enjoy size and seniority while you have it, because the day is coming real soon when all you'll have over us is a deflated ego and the memories of when you were taller and stronger."

"Yeah, yeah. Don't rub it in." William grimaced, accepting the help of his eldest son while reaching out to ruffle his hair. "At least I'm still taller."

"Are you sure?" Jesse eyed him down nose to nose.

Emma laughed as the wind blew Jesse's hair up, making him taller than his father, who was beginning to substantially lose what was left of his blond mane.

"It's official. Your son is now taller by . . . about a hair." Emma reached up using her index finger and thumb as a measuring device on her son's locks, showing just how much taller Jesse—with the help of his hair—had grown than his father.

"Hey, that's a low blow," William accused.

"No, my dear. A low blow would make our son shorter by a hair rather than taller," Emma countered with a laugh. William put his arm around Emma's shoulder as she was letting McKenna go so she could chase after her brothers, who were headed back up the trail toward their grandparents.

Emma watched as her two older boys helped Jeanie, William's mother, down a rather rocky part of the trail while Walter, William's father, stopped to pluck a magical coin out of Jaden's ear. He then gave it to a delighted McKenna, who lovingly barreled into her grandpa's right knee, rendering him off balance.

It's a good thing Jaden's there with his quick reflexes to grab him, thought Emma as she imagined Walter landing unceremoniously on his backside. Walter merely laughed at his lack of grace and scooped up his lively granddaughter, tickling her little ribs.

Emma smiled, knowing a painful tush for Walter had been averted. She dearly loved that man—and her mother-in-law too, for that matter. Emma's parents lived several states away, and rising airfare costs and her father's terrible night vision, coupled with her mother's nervousness about his driving, made their visits a rarity. And since Emma had married and had children, the same high airfares and lack of time off of work for William made visits more rare than any of them would have liked. But Walter and Jeanie had made her feel such a part of their family from the day she'd met William that her ache at being on her own had quickly vanished.

William quickly pulled her meandering mind back to the present. "At least you're still shorter." He grinned while standing just a little bit taller.

Emma laughed. "You'll always be my knight in shining armor, even if that armor did come from the boys' department at Wal-Mart."

"Hey, I resent that. I moved up to preteens the year we were married."

"Yeah, but haven't you heard? It's a fact that you shrink with age—that is, except for your feet and ears. They, along with the inches on your waistband and the rogue hair in your nostrils, ears, and eyebrows, continue to grow until the day you die."

William put his arm around her shoulders and pulled her closer. "My dear, you're not making age sound very appealing. If what you say is true, then I'm going to end up looking like a Mr. Potato Head with Andy Rooney eyebrows. Maybe death while you're young isn't so tragic after all . . ."

Emma stepped out from under his arm and faced him. "Hey, don't even kid about that! You may be overly sensitive ever since your brother pointed out that you're only five-eleven and three-quarters instead of the six feet you've always claimed to be, but you're always going to be my own personal gentle giant."

The sudden change in topic had all too suddenly brought a lump to Emma's throat and tears to her eyes. How could she ever live without her sweet William? She bent to retrieve the patchwork quilt before her emotions got the better of her and ruined what was left of her already smudged mascara.

William placed his hand on her shoulder and pulled her back into his embrace, wiping away the tears clinging to her lower lashes. "Hey, I was only kidding. You know that neither heaven nor earth could keep me away from you and the kids."

"Do you promise?" Emma asked while scrutinizing his face for any signs of deception or uncertainty. "Promise you'll always be here for us?"

William's face softened even more as he held up three fingers and stiffly saluted. "Scouts honor." He then took the blanket from her and continued, "I can't imagine anywhere I'd rather be than here on this earth with you. The best is yet to come, Em. The best it yet to come. And even if some mystical force did try to separate us, I promise you some-how, someway, I'd find a way to let you know that I wasn't far off."

Emma sat in the dark of her living room, watching the storm raging outside. A few years back, a night like this would have been welcomed in peaceful solitude as she gratefully snuggled up, knowing her family was close at hand and sheltered from the elements. But as Emma thought about the eight-by-four patch of land located at the base of the mountains exposed to the harsh and bitter winds, she couldn't help but let her tears fall so that they matched the downward stream of wet, heavy snowflakes outside.

Even though Emma's more rational side knew that her dearly loved husband was well beyond feeling the bitter cold as he rested beneath the frozen earth, the emotional, tender side of her still instinctively yearned to care for him. Emma patted her soggy cheeks with a quilt corner and then rested her head upon her covered, drawn-up knees. She hated the feeling of sheer helplessness that had come with William's death.

The phone rang. Emma picked up the handset and looked at the caller-ID display. Quickly recognizing the North Carolina area code, Emma put the phone back on the couch, unable to face the cheeriness of her mother's voice as she suggested her daughter do this or that. Emma had already heard one too many times, "But, honey, you have to get on with your life. William wouldn't want you to give up on life." But it didn't matter how many gems of well-meant advice were given; Emma's thoughts and heart clung to William. And despite the droves of good-intentioned people who tried to pull her back to the present, Emma knew she would forever remain his.

She lifted her chin to look out the window again and sighed heavily. "Oh, Will . . . I guess covering your grave with Grandma's quilt won't quite cut it tonight," she said into the darkness, pulling the well-worn flannel patches tighter around herself. "It wouldn't do a thing for you, and I'd probably freeze to death if I laid down beside you wanting to be close for a minute."

While looking at the portrait (taken just eighteen months before) hanging above their family mission statement, which

Emma had stenciled on the entryway wall, tears again welled up as she studied the smiling faces full of bright hope in a future full of opportunities. Emma turned away from the portrait and sighed.

"But I guess someone has to stay behind for the children. They need at least one parent to help them through this trial we call life."

If only she knew how to do it. The accident had placed challenges in Emma's life that she felt completely unprepared for. Besides the financial aspects (not only had the driver who'd hit William been severely intoxicated but was uninsured as well), Emma, who'd been a stay-at-home mom since the birth of her first child, was struggling to balance the demands of her four children and having to earn an income. Had it not been for their good friend Paul's assistance in getting her the job she had, homelessness would be another addition to her list of woes.

But even with all her hours at work earning a decent wage and after paying the medical and funeral bills with William's life insurance benefits, there was very little left to cover the needs of her family, let alone to provide much of a Christmas for them. And she didn't see things getting much better in the short term, or the long run either.

But as one who'd usually found a way to count her blessings, Emma couldn't help but thank God that her oldest son, Jesse, at the tender age of seventeen, had taken his studies seriously with the intent to graduate early and in the process had earned a full-ride scholarship to a small eastern college. Emma struggled to be happy for him, although the thoughts of him moving on—even though deep down she wouldn't want it any other way—just about killed her. He'd been so responsible, becoming her rock and the voice of reason when she'd felt just about ready to crack. And unfortunately those times had become more and more frequent with the pressures of being (in Emma's perception anyway) an ill-equipped single parent who was consumed with trying to meet all of her family's needs.

Furthering her guilt was the fact that her next two sons, Michael, now fourteen, and Jaden, now twelve, had taken on more responsibility than two young teens should ever have had to handle. Where Emma had always been the one to happily take care of the yard, laundry, food preparation, and taxi service to practices and extracurricular activities, her sons now had to be the ones taking over laundry, cooking, cleanup, and yard work after a full day of school and with homework waiting. They too knew that their only chance at a college education was through scholarships. Had it not been for good friends who'd taken on the financial burden of team dues and scout costs, and for getting them to and from practices and other activities, her sons wouldn't have had a life at all. Emma once again thanked God for this blessing, even though she had to push aside her guilt for hardly ever being able to watch or support them at their games.

At least the older boys were old enough to understand their unfortuitous circumstances . . . but six-year-old McKenna—she still harbored perfect childlike faith that even though Heavenly Father had taken her daddy, the world was still a just and kind place where fates were balanced and, in the end, the good ultimately outweighed the bad. McKenna, loving the magic that Christmas offered, knew with all her heart that Santa was one of those scales helping to balance the fates. And, as such, she was absolutely positive that he'd be bringing her and her family something extra special this year.

Emma struggled with how to explain to her sweet little girl that Santa was only for those who could afford him. His joviality was saved for those whose worldly cares were less than the dollars acquired to pay the bills and whose obligations weren't stretched beyond what a mere twenty-four hours could supply.

Emma could barely stand the thought of looking into McKenna's eyes as she watched the innocence associated with Christmas fall from them forever. Emma dreaded McKenna's disappointment on Christmas morning when she would be catapulted into a cruel reality beyond what she'd already endured, a reality that pulled fiercely at Emma's heart, making her feel even more like a failure.

Emma unwrapped herself from the faded patchwork quilt, picked up the last ornament off the coffee table, and went to place it on the tree. She held it up, using the tree lights for background illumination, and examined it closely. This one had always been her favorite because it perfectly melded all that was important about the season. She ran her finger along the trestles of the delicate glass shelter that housed Santa kneeling reverently, hat in hand, by the Christ child's manger. Jolly Old Saint Nick—who'd been created through the hope and innocence of giving and believing in miracles—looked upon the babe with adoration, respect, gratitude, and tender love.

Emma held on to it for just a moment longer before whispering almost inaudibly to no one in particular as she placed it in its customary eye-level position on the front of the artificial tree, "If only it could be so simple."

She then turned and retrieved her blanket before heading upstairs, where she would once again curl up with it in the comfort of her room. She closed her eyes while she imagined William close by before burying her head in his pillow and inhaling the faint, familiar scent of his cologne while crying herself to sleep.

He watched through the big picture window that was framed by the Spanish archway from the shadows of the front porch. It had indeed been a tough year for Emma and her family, but he knew if he could do this right, it would be one of the most unforgettable Christmases she and the children would ever have. Resolute in his resolve, he tugged at the collar of his thick winter jacket and tiptoed in his black leather boots back through what was left of the children's footprints in the front yard. When he reached the light post down the street, he stopped a moment to look up at the swirling snow before glancing back at the eerie blue reflections cast from TV images in Emma's room. He smiled, squared his shoulders, and headed off into the darkness.

Emma woke early that morning after another restless night's sleep. She'd hoped that by having the droning noise of late-night infomercials on, her thoughts would wash away and quit tormenting her so that peaceful slumber would be a possibility. No such luck. After once again recognizing that her current state was not, in fact, a nightmare and that a rather somber reality awaited her, which included her job at the Rocky Mountain Counseling and Family Services Center, she flipped her covers off and stumbled to her vanity.

"Wow, you look a sight," Emma said to her reflection before flushing her face with frigid water, hoping that some of the redness and swelling from another night of sobbing might dissipate.

Just like every other morning, Emma went through the motions of getting herself ready for work before waking the kids. She looked once more at the sad figure in the mirror and nodded her acquiescence. She was nothing flashy, but at least she was presentable. "All the better to blend in and get through another day," she mused as she put her keys in her purse and put on a happy face before heading down the hall to wake her children.

"Rise and shine, you sleepy heads! Daylight's a wastin'," Emma called as she opened the blinds, flooding each of their rooms with sunlight. "Come on! We've got another day to tackle, and whoever's at the table last does the dishes."

The three older boys rolled out of bed amid grumbles, yawns, and stretches and headed toward the bathrooms. Emma snuck into McKenna's room and sat on the edge of her bed, staring at her daughter. McKenna tried to suppress a smile as she pretended to be asleep.

"You can't fool me, missy. I see that smirk," Emma said while tickling the little girl's nose with the tip of her own long, blonde braid.

"How'd ya know?" McKenna giggled, bringing her knees up to her chest to protect her ribs as her mother reached beneath the covers to tickle her.

"Oh, I don't know. Maybe it was that smirk you were trying so hard to hide or your eyelids fluttering while you tried to sneak peeks," Emma countered as she pulled Kenna's eyelet-lace comforter down before selecting her clothes from the closet. "I want you to hurry today, sweetheart. Okay?"

"Mama, when will Daddy be home for Christmas?" Emma froze with her hands on a green plaid jumper. It took a moment before she could face her daughter.

"Why would you ask that, sweetie?"

"Because in my dream, he said he'd be here with us."

"Oh, honey, it was just a dream. You know Daddy is in heaven looking over us."

"I know, but when he visited me last night in my dream, he said that he'd be here for Christmas and that he was sending a special present so that we'd know what Christmas is like in heaven and what it can be like here too."

"Wow . . . That must've been quite a dream."

"So, when is he coming?" pressed McKenna.

Emma didn't have the patience or the stomach for this right now. There were things to do and schedules to keep. And although Emma would've loved nothing more than to slip into a fantasy so she could delude herself into believing that the magic of Christmas was real, she'd already shed enough tears the previous night over life's realities, and her eyes were still burning from the salt.

To even tease McKenna's hope with this line of questioning would do nothing more than hasten the demise of her dreams, making Emma sob again over her inadequacies as a mother and as a surrogate father. She could already feel another batch of fresh tears being wrestled from her aching heart. Yes, thought Emma, it would be much better to put the conversation off until she could dignify her child's question with a decorum of stability mixed with tenderness.

"Kenna, we'll talk about this later. Why don't you think about your dream a little more and tell me what you've come up with after I get home from work, okay? Now let's hurry and get dressed so no one will be late today."

McKenna knew her mother's terse response meant that she was not going to get anywhere on the subject at the moment. That was okay though. Pretty soon everything would be better because she knew Daddy was coming for a visit and they'd be able to celebrate Christmas with him.

Michael was the first one to arrive home and see the envelope propped up against the door. His feet stopped. Immediately, his keen and inquisitive mind began to size it up. It was not your standard everyday envelope. It was an odd size—more square than rectangular—and made of a bright, heavy-duty red paper with bumps on it. He bounded the rest of the way up the front walk and swooped to pick it up. As he looked a little closer at the paper, he realized that the bumps were actually embossed pictures of presents wrapped with big fancy bows. He studied the curly, fancy handwriting that spelled out "The Jensens" and wondered why there was no return address. He turned the envelope over. Where the flap came to a point was a seal with two letters imprinted into a blob of green wax: *SC*. Under that, in the same ornate handwriting as the front of the envelope, was a tiny note on the bottom edge. "Do not open until the whole family is together," it instructed. After thoroughly scrutinizing the envelope, he held it up to his ear and shook it. He jumped when Jaden, who had sneaked up from the curb, poked him in the ribs.

"Jeez, I didn't even hear you come up the walk."

"Ha! I got you." Jaden reveled in his momentary success before noticing the object of Michael's attention. "So, what is it?" He reached for the envelope, but Michael snatched it away before Jaden could take possession.

"I don't know. There aren't many clues and no return address."

"Let's go steam it open, read it, and then seal it back up so no one will ever know we snooped."

"Are you an idiot? See this wax seal here? It won't come off with steam. You have to break it to get inside, and there's no way to do that without everyone knowing you disobeyed the instructions."

"It was just a thought . . ."

"If we want to know what it is, there's only one thing to do," Michael said as he unlocked the door and took the lead, knocking a picture off the wall in his hurried race to the phone.

Emma waded through the traffic as she wound her way home. She thought about the mysterious envelope the boys had called her about. It made her uneasy that someone was visiting their house while she was not there to protect her home and family. But since she was a mother whose lot in life it was to be the sole provider, she had no choice other than to take every precaution possible and teach her children about safety. And if that wasn't enough, she prayed that since she couldn't be there to personally watch over them, maybe William could.

As she pulled into the driveway, McKenna bounded out the door, waving the red envelope. "Look, Mama. Someone brought us a surprise!"

"Let me see, Kenna." Emma took the envelope and looked for a postmark. There was none. She looked at her watch, which displayed the current date—December 13—and noted with sadness that it had been almost a full year since the accident.

"Well, shall we go in, Kenna, and get the boys so we can eat dinner? I think everyone must be hungry by now. And then we can figure out what to do with this letter."

Emma had spent almost every moment of dinner trying to decide what she should do with the letter. Should she allow the kids to open it? Should she divert their attention and throw it away? Life as of late had brought them a lot of surprises, and none of them had been nice. Call it being jaded or merely cautious, either way Emma wanted to shield her children from any more "surprises."

But after eating, cleaning up after dinner, and thoroughly interrogating the boys about the broken picture frame, which now had a mishmash of clear tape holding its glass together, they were still focused on the mystery letter. Emma felt that she had no other choice than to let them open it. She didn't want to be the one to disappoint them again. It would be better if a complete stranger did it rather than their own mother. So after carefully weighing her options, Emma took control of the situation as best she could and gathered her family in the living room by the tree to break the seal on the letter. After cautiously scrutinizing it for any unknown substances, smells, or sounds, she carefully extracted the paper folded neatly inside. The handwriting was framed by tiny ornaments that made a perfect snow globe scene. Its words were written in the same elaborate penmanship found on the front of the envelope.

"Well, what's it say?" asked Jesse, anxious to get back to his studies.

Emma cleared her throat and began . . .

Dear Jensens,

I know that this year has been a difficult one for you. You have dealt with numerous challenges and faced many of your biggest fears, and, yet, in light of it all, whether you know it or not, you have managed to become stronger as you've focused on what's really important.

You have strived to live up to your family's mission statement, which is written upon your wall:

To see God's face is our only hope
And to be there as a family, our only goal,
For we can think of no greater nobility
Than to be with each other for eternity.

You have made sacrifices, supported each other, and clung to a hope that heaven is not so very far away after all. Even I would be hard pressed to give you anything of more value than you yourselves have already managed to obtain.

But as the Christmas season has grown closer, I've also noticed that there is sadness, a burden that has become too heavy to bear on your own. And so as I've watched over you while checking in to see that you've remained "nice," I decided that rather than the traditional gifts of toys and "stuff," I wanted to give you a Christmas to savor. One that would help you remember what the true gifts of the season are.

Christmas, when broken down, takes Christ's name and the shortened Middle English form of the word masse, which means "festival" or "celebration," and clearly defines Christmas as a celebration of Christ. It's also interesting to note that the word mas in many of the old languages means "more." So, this Christmas season, my dear family, will be a celebration where I will bring more of Christ into the holiday as you celebrate his life and example.

Every day I will deliver a few items in a box along with a letter detailing your instructions for an activity meant to teach you the true meaning and gifts of Christmas. Once you have emptied your Christmas box, set it back on the front porch behind the bench.

It is my sincere hope that you enjoy these holiday offerings before allowing too many of life's treasures to pass you by. I hope you will remember the true meaning of Christmas and what it means to be a forever family, especially as you come to the end of this—the most difficult of years.

I am proud of you and the progress you have thus far made and send my blessings as well as my love as you embark upon this journey together, learning, growing, and knowing even better what you already believe.

Loving always,
Santa

Emma looked around the room. "Do any of you know who this is from?" She was met with blank stares . . . except from McKenna.

"Duh, Mom. It's from Santa. See, it says so right there." She pointed to the unfamiliar signature and then, as if a memory had sparked the light in her eyes, she jumped up with excitement and faced her mother.

"This is it! This is what Daddy was talking about," she babbled.

Jesse and Michael looked at each other quizzically while Jaden simply rolled his eyes and hummed the theme from *Close Encounters of the Third Kind*. Emma gave him a stern look and then turned to her daughter.

"What do you mean, sweetheart?"

"My dream last night. Daddy said he was sending a special surprise to help us remember all about Christmas. This is it! He sent us Santa!"

Emma reached for her little girl. "Oh, sweetie, I don't think Daddy would—"

"Yes, he would! Because you are so sad and he knows that we need a good Christmas and he wants us all to be happy! You'll see. Daddy and Santa are going to make it the best Christmas ever!" And with that McKenna grabbed the envelope, hugged it to her chest, and twirled in wide circles while saying, "Thank you, Santa! And I love you, Daddy! Merry Christmas to you both."

Dazed, the boys watched her gleefully tromp up the stairs to bed. Did she actually know something, or had she finally lost her marbles? Jaden was sure he knew the answer. He looped his index finger to the side of his head, indicating that his younger sister had gone cuckoo. Emma, on the other hand, looked at her feet and chewed on her lower lip as her stomach churned with uneasiness. She tallied the impossible situation placed before her. This was the cruelest of jokes— to let a little girl believe, even if it was unbeknownst to the sender, that her father would be able to visit for Christmas and that Santa was doing his bidding. How was Emma ever going to repair the fresh heartbreak this charade would surely cause her daughter? Not only would her father never make an appearance, but McKenna would also find hardly any gifts under the tree on Christmas morning. If there was one thing Emma had come to know for sure, it was that, as hard as she tried at times, she was no miracle worker.

He watched the scene unfold through the big picture window from the darkness across the street. No one would even have known he was there had it not been for the puffs of condensation escaping as he exhaled. Almost as if he could hear the tumultuous emotions swirling in Emma's mind, he smiled and whispered to himself, "Miracles do happen this time of year, Emma. This whole season is about miracles, and, if I play my cards right, the biggest miracle you'll come to enjoy over the next few days is that of peace."

He then pulled his hat a little lower over his brow, bending into the wind rather than trying to reach his full height like he normally did, and headed off in the opposite direction whistling "Silent Night."

Emma did not have to wake any of her children the next morning. McKenna, in her excitement, had woken everyone up as she loudly practiced the songs from her school's Christmas program while cleaning her room and putting away her pajamas after dressing. Emma peered from around the doorway.

"You're up early. What gives?"

"Santa's watching. I bet Daddy is too, and if they're going to be watching us every day, I'm going to be a really good girl so the surprises'll keep coming. I wanna know what Christmas in heaven is like."

"Kenna, honey, don't get your hopes up too high. Sometimes the fantasies we create in our mind turn out very different from what actually happens. I don't want you to be disappointed and end up hating Christmas."

"Oh, Mama, you'll see. Daddy never breaks his promises, and he promised he'd make this the best Christmas ever!"

Emma turned away and went back into her room so that her daughter couldn't see the deep furrows forming in her brow. "That's what I once thought too." Emma sighed and closed her bedroom door.

"I'm telling you, it was the weirdest thing." Jesse ran his fingers through his hair and looked at Tina, his advanced chemistry lab partner. "It's like Kenna knew something absolute, like someone was standing right there in front of her and she had no doubts whatsoever."

"I guess that's why they always talk about the faith of a child. It's perfect and absolute," Tina said as she poured her solution into a beaker and heated it over their Bunsen burner.

"It's not Kenna I worry about though—it's Mom. That letter seemed to stress her out even more than she already is. I know it's just about killing her that she can't do much for us this Christmas, but she reacted almost like it was a letter bomb or tainted with anthrax."

"Well, that's probably because the thought of someone watching your family and dropping by every night to peer in your windows freaks her out."

"Yeah, I guess you're right. I never thought of it that way. I guess I'll have to be extra careful about keeping the doors locked and watching for strangers lurking around."

"Don't spoil the surprises . . ."

"I won't. I just don't want there to be any more lousy shockers. She deserves a break." Jesse's serious grimace belied any confidence that he, as the man of the house, could keep his family safe. He shook his head, finished mixing his part of the solution, and added it to the beaker Tina was heating.

Jaden casually looked up and down the street, making sure he'd beaten Michael home from school before heading to the mailbox. Every day had become a race since the two had forged an agreement stipulating that the first one home got their pick of daily chores. Jaden was still grinning ear to ear over his clever new shortcut home when he heard Michael call from the corner, "You'd better run, you twerp, or you might lose your chance!"

"Holy mother of monkeys," Jaden mumbled to himself as he slammed the mailbox shut and ran up the front steps while pulling his key from his pocket. "I'm not cleaning toilets and toothpaste again," he vowed.

He came to a screeching halt, though, before he rammed into the packages that were blocking the front door.

"Why'd ya st—Oooh, I see." Michael's confusion turned to comprehension as he saw the reason for Jaden's abrupt halt. He sauntered forward, taking in the stack of packages. There on top was another red envelope just like the first. On the front was the same ornate handwriting. Having momentarily put aside their competitive urges, the brothers riffled through the packages.

There was a bundle of wood tied with a red ribbon, a white cotton drawstring bag filled with a few more items, and a circular box with Christmas scenes painted in muted colors—almost like a dream sequence—all around the sides. On the lid was a picture of an old-fashioned Christmas tree with soft, delicate branches. There was a gold carrying cord with a tag attached explicitly commanding, "Do not open until you are together as a family."

Jaden picked up as much as he could and bounded through the front door, leaving the rest to Michael's care.

After dumping his armload by the tree in the living room, he taunted Michael that he'd still beat him though the door and then raced down the hall to call their mother.

Emma quickly rushed home after work, anxious to see what the containers held. According to her brothers, McKenna had been chattering incessantly about the delivery since she'd gotten home from school. Although Emma was certain this charade would ultimately end up in disappointment for her daughter, Emma had to admit that, at least for the moment, it was nice seeing the light of enthusiasm in her daughter's eyes again. It hadn't been very bright since the night her daddy had died. Emma sighed. "What harm can it do to play along if even for just one night . . ."

After the dishes had been cleared and cleaned, Emma and the children retired to the living room, where, by the light of the tree, they opened their letter.

Jensen Family,

When a child is born, a mother's first instinct is to wrap her precious new baby in warmth, whether in a blanket, in her arms, or, as in your Savior's case, swaddling clothes.

Warmth is much more than a physical need, however. It is the feeling you get when the Spirit has touched you. It's how you feel when you are at peace with the world. It's that feeling you get when you curl up under your blankets at night after another good day of hard work.

The first gift of Christmas you get to celebrate as a family is warmth in all of its forms. Within this box are some items to help you rejoice in feeling safe and sound here in your home. There is food to warm you from within as you enjoy the good feelings that come from being part of a loving family who sticks with you through thick and thin. You'll also find something to physically comfort you when you need a little extra warmth.

As you gather around the fire, you will share your thoughts about a Savior who gave up some of these simple comforts so that you could bask in the warmth of your Father in Heaven once more.

Jensens, this season think about what warmth really means to you and how blessed you are to have it in so many ways this holiday season. May the glow of the true meaning of Christmas continue to warm your hearts this year, and may his light continue to shine brightly over you, keeping you safe and secure from the harshness and cruelty of a sometimes rather cold world.

I love you, which is why I want you to know warmth tonight.

Loving always,
Santa

P.S. All of you be home by 5:30 p.m. tomorrow night dressed in nice clothes and ready to go.

Emma settled back into the couch cushion, trying to decipher her thoughts. But before she could make heads or tails out of any of them, her children had quickly jumped into laying out the rest of the evening before them.

Jesse carefully untied the drawstring on the cotton bag and started pulling out the items housed inside. There was a box of graham crackers, a bag of marshmallows, a canister of hot chocolate, and a package of chocolate bars.

"Can I open the other box?" asked Jaden, already fidgeting with the lid.

"Yeah, I want to see what's inside! Please, Mama, let him . . ." begged McKenna.

"Oh, all right, go ahead, Jaden." Emma nodded her

approval while fighting with the nervousness she felt over the possibility of impending disappointment.

Jaden lifted the lid off the box and pitched it aside. In wide-eyed wonder, he began pulling out the softest blankets he'd ever felt.

"This one must be mine," McKenna squealed as she reached over Jaden's shoulder to grab a pink one with white hearts and lace around the edges. She held it to her cheek and whirled so the blanket could wrap itself around her small body as she fell back onto the couch.

Jaden tossed a red plaid one to Jesse, knowing that red was his favorite color, before grabbing the next one—which was green and decorated with hockey equipment—and slung it across his shoulders.

Michael didn't wait for Jaden to distribute the last two. He reached into the box and pulled out a blue blanket adorned with stars, moons, and log cabins. It was followed by an ivory quilt with scalloped edges and a large star design in shades of green (Emma's favorite color) in the middle and smaller ones that lined the edges.

"This reminds me of the camping trips we used to go on with Dad and Grandpa at the old abandoned homestead." Michael reminisced as he touched one of the small cabins and let a smile creep across his face. "What do you think of yours, Mom?"

Emma ran a finger across the perfect stitching knowing how long it must've taken. "I-I don't know what to say . . . It's beautiful."

Jesse stepped in and took charge of the night by placing the items by the fireplace before heading into the kitchen to fetch some matches and an old paper. Michael, the family's self-appointed campfire master, arranged the logs on the grate while Jaden, moved by his constant hunger and love of chocolate, ran to get some wire coat hangers to fashion into marshmallow toasting skewers.

Once everyone had consumed their fill of s'mores and hot chocolate, Jesse broached the assigned subject matter and opened the conversation with what he'd learned in his Sunday school class the previous week.

"Did you know that Mary and Joseph had to go to Bethlehem because they were descendants of King David? If Caesar hadn't risen to power, Joseph could have been a king. Joseph, a king through bloodlines, was chosen to be the stepfather to the king of Jews, and yet both father and son ended up in such a humble situation on one of the greatest nights in the world's history."

"That was no accident," countered Emma thoughtfully. "Christ chose to be born in the lowliest of circumstances so he could rise above those conditions and ascend to the highest position of all, next to God, his Father, and be an example to those of us who need hope, direction, and a path to follow. He wanted us to know that no matter where we are on the spectrum of existence, his understanding and compassion are limitless because he's been there."

Even as she spoke, it was the first time Emma had really listened to the concepts she'd been taught ever since childhood. She'd never completely understood them before, but tonight she got an inkling of what it meant to know that the man whose birth she was celebrating truly understood her pain, her loneliness, her fears, and her discouragements.

After everyone had shared their thoughts and feelings and was enjoying a contented silence, Emma looked into their sleepy eyes and realized that it was time to break the magic of the evening.

"Time for bed, you sleepy heads. Last one up does the dishes in the morning."

They all pattered upstairs, but Emma remained on the couch, wrapped in her old patchwork quilt as she ran her fingers along the stitching of her new one. She smiled. It had been a nice evening. One that, for the first time in a long while, had not been encumbered by the stresses of her life. She might even be so bold as to say that she'd felt a sliver of peace while sitting in front of the fire with her family. Tonight she resolved that she would not hug her quilt while crying herself to sleep. Instead, still purposely plotting her course, she'd thank God for the warmth she'd felt this one night.

Emma hadn't slept that soundly in a long time. She yawned and stretched, getting the creaks out of her system before jumping out of bed and checking in on her children. She smiled to see every one of them wrapped up snuggly with their blankets. She almost hated to disturb their dreams.

"No harm in letting them sleep a few more minutes," she decided as she headed into her bathroom to shower.

"Hey there, shorty," Michael called to his brother in the seventh-grade section of the cafeteria as he passed through to his normal seat in the ninth-grade section. "Better eat your Wheaties if you have any hopes of beating me home to see what's on the doorstep." Their rivalry had suddenly become more about being the first to the Santa letters than about having the best picks on the chore chart.

Jaden dropped his tray off at the cleanup window, and his friends followed him over to where Michael sat with his own friends. "Yeah well, they always say as you get older, you get slower," taunted Jaden as he crossed his arms across his chest and looked side to side at his seventh grade companions for support and approval.

"And wisdom will always win the race. Haven't you heard of the tortoise and the hare?" Michael countered amid the laughter of his friends.

"Age before wisdom, my brother. You may have age, but I guess that leaves wisdom to the younger. Oh," Jaden exaggeratedly plucked a hair off of Michael's shoulder, "could this be an omen that you'll lose by a 'hair'?"

Michael shook his head, laughing, and then quipped as he watched the last of Jaden's posse catch up, "We'll see who gets there first. Oh look, it's Tyler." Michael nodded in the direction of Jaden's best friend. "If you go with him after school, I just may be sittin' on the porch all alone waiting for hours for you to show up," he said, remembering what had transpired three weeks earlier when Jaden had accepted a ride from Tyler's older brother, hoping to be the victor in the race home.

"Ha ha, really funny. It wasn't my fault that Jeremy decided to stop by his girlfriend's house."

"Yeah well, if you weren't ruled by your stomach and the promise of chocolate, you couldn't have been so easily bribed into being his convenient excuse to take the car. Eight hours for a candy bar—you hold the record."

Tyler, hearing the last of the conversation, piped in. "In Jaden's defense, Jeremy said he was just going to take us to the store real quick and finally make good on the bet we won beating him in basketball. He didn't let either of us know we'd be held captive while he made goo-goo eyes at Julie."

"Either way, I got off chore duty that night, and little brother here is now known as the kid who almost gave Mom a heart attack."

"Shut up. I still feel pretty bad about making her worry so much." Jaden sulked at the memory of Emma rushing out the door to embrace him before following up with the scolding of a lifetime.

"Good thing. Your guilt has come in pretty handy for me as of late!" Michael slapped his brother on the shoulder and turned to socialize with his friends.

As much as he hated to admit it, it was true. Michael

would recount the miniscule details of what they'd kiddingly come to call "Mom's night of terror," and Jaden's guilt would push him into doing an extra-good job at his chores and, on certain occasions, even taking on an additional chore or two. It would be so much easier if he could quit having a conscience, he lamented as he headed off to gym class.

Both Jaden and Michael raced out the school doors to beat the other one home, but as they were heading for a photo finish at the doorstep, they were stopped short by Jesse, who was already there holding the Santa letter and carrying the box inside.

"Why are you home so early?" quizzed Michael.

Jesse worked as a student aid in the chemistry lab at his school. The opportunity provided him a bit of extra pocket cash while furthering his studies. "Labs were cancelled—something about an experiment gone wrong. None of us could stand the smell."

Jaden didn't care why Jesse was home. He was too focused on the latest Santa delivery. "Can we sneak a peek?" he inquired.

"No. We go on the honor system in this house—something I pray every day you'll learn the meaning of," Jesse nonchalantly chided while browsing through the mail before discreetly slipping his hand behind his back to accept a celebratory high-five from Michael for his quick wit.

But before their younger brother could rightly defend himself, the door burst open. "Is it here? Is it here?" yelled McKenna.

Jesse picked up his little sister and diverted her attention while Michael set the items back behind the tree. "Is what here?"

"Our Santa letter. Has he brought it yet? I know it's going to be something extra special 'cause he told us all to be home by a certain time. Where is it?"

"Oooohhh, that! Well you see, I think we were getting the neighbor's mail by mistake . . ."

"Don't tease me, Jess. The letters have our names on them, and Daddy wouldn't send them to anyone else. I'm pretty smart for my age, you know, so you can't fool me easy." She wiggled from Jesse's grasp and ran into the living room by the tree. It took her only a moment to find them half hidden behind the branches. Once she'd made sure the delivery was there, she rushed to the phone to call her mother, reminding her to be home on time.

Gathered round the tree, Emma and the children opened the next letter.

Jensen Family,

When Christ was born, music filled the galaxy. All of heaven and earth sang, heralding his long-awaited arrival. No event has ever been more anticipated and celebrated, save his next coming, than the birth of our Savior.

Music is the language of the heart. While words touch the mind, it is the music that touches the heart—the combination of the two touches the soul.

Music is how we celebrate, rejoice, express our anguish, honor others with praise, and worship with humility, reverence, and gratitude.

Music was one of the first things that heralded our Savior's birth, and it is one of the best ways to bring the spirit of Christmas joy into our homes. Think back to the Christmases before this one—while you put up the decorations you listened to your favorite Christmas carols and hummed along. Where music is the dominant voice, anger and screaming are not heard. When one sings songs of praise and joy, he cannot also speak vile words of hate and prejudice.

Tonight you will have the opportunity to listen to some of the most beautiful voices in the world singing some of the most treasured songs of the season. Here are some tickets to the Christmas concert at Kingston Hall. There are enough for your whole family to go.

After listening to these wonderful songs while spending time with your family, you will come home in front of your fireplace once again and share as a family. You will discuss your favorite carols and songs and why they mean so much to you.

I love you, which is why tonight I want you to enjoy the gift of beautiful music.

Loving always,
Santa

Emma opened the box and looked at the five tickets inside. Although this was a free Christmas concert put on every year, it was next to impossible to get tickets because of the limited seating in the concert hall. Those who didn't have access to the Internet would line up hours in advance for a chance to get the few held at the box office. And those who could get them online pounced a minute before the "ticket lines" opened, praying they'd be lucky enough to get what was needed before the tickets were gone in just minutes. She and William had tried without luck for the last three years to get some for their family. How in the world had their mysterious benefactor managed to get the coveted tickets—and five at that?

"Well, I guess we shouldn't look a gift horse in the mouth," Emma finally decided and hurried the kids up the stairs to get ready. She stopped on the third stair and looked at the piano, which had sat silent ever since William's passing. She smiled, remembering William playing songs and making up goofy lyrics to amuse the children. He had actually proposed to her in such a way—with an absurd song in front of their friends at a party.

It had been a long time since she had really opened her heart to the sweet sound of lyrical notes and allowed them to caress her soul. As she turned to head up the stairs, she found herself thinking that for the first time in a long, long time, she was actually excited to go somewhere and enjoy the sound of music.

McKenna woke up bright and early Friday morning, happily humming songs from the selection she'd heard the night before. As McKenna slid out of her bed and into her mouse slippers, she grabbed her bathrobe off her bedpost, put it on, and twirled and sashayed into her mother's room.

"Morning, Mama. Did you have sweet dreams last night?"

"Sweet enough to eat. They were of you, my little one," Emma teased as she reached for her little girl and pretended to nibble at her ribs.

After a bit more tickling, McKenna pulled back with a thoughtful look. "Daddy used to do that. He'd tease me that he was hungry for some baby ribs."

"He did do that, didn't he? Does it bother you if I do it?"

"No, I like seeing you laugh again. And when we do the things he used to do, it makes me feel like he's not very far away."

Emma smiled and hugged her daughter. Ironically, for that very reason, Emma had avoided doing the things that William had done or even participating in anything that reminded her of him. Subconsciously, she had rationalized that if she could keep him out of sight, she'd be able to keep him out of mind. Emma was quickly coming to realize, however, that the exact opposite was true. The more she tried to avoid any remembrance of him, the more she felt alienated from him and missed him terribly. Funny how her six-year-old could understand a lesson so uncomplicated and yet so profound.

Emma pulled her little girl back into her embrace and, with a hint of shame, lowered her gaze and kissed the crown of McKenna's head. It was sad that it had taken a child's wisdom to explain to Emma a concept so simple. She gave herself credit, though, for the one lesson she was finally coming to understand—that to take the sting out of death was to take the love out of life, and to do so would ultimately be the greater evil to bear.

"I loved how they sang our favorite songs last night."

"Whose favorite songs?"

"Mine and yours and Daddy's."

"And what would those be?"

"I like the Mary song when it talks about her baby."

"I think it's called 'Mary, Did You Know?' " offered Emma.

"Yeah, I think so too." McKenna sighed. "Do you think she did know?"

"Know what exactly?"

"That baby Jesus would do so many cool things and be such a good person?"

"Well, I think she had a notion that he was very special. But she was so young and innocent when he was born that I don't think she quite understood the importance of his mission or the pain she herself would have to bear while supporting him as he accomplished what he was sent here to do."

"Do you think when Jesus died it hurt Mary as much as it hurt you when Daddy died?"

The question caught Emma off guard, and she had to take a moment to think about it. How would a mother's grief compare to that of a wife? The only comparison Emma had was that of her mother-in-law Jeanie's grief. It had just about killed Jeanie to say good-bye to her only son. Emma had opted more and more to stay away, thinking that having her and the children around would only add to Jeanie's anguish. But somewhere deep inside, Emma knew that it was looking into Jeanie's eyes, a landscape painted by sorrow that mirrored her own, that kept her visits at bay. She forced her thoughts back to Mary.

How could the young woman have borne raising a son and nurturing him, all the while knowing what he was sent to accomplish? Emma's mind once again gravitated back to her own circumstances. Could Emma herself have married William had she known this would be her lot? For the first time in her life, Emma thought about Mary the child, Mary the mother, and Mary the strong and able woman. If Emma herself could only have that kind of strength . . .

McKenna broke into Emma's swirling thoughts. "Mama?"

"I'm sorry, hon. I was just thinking about your question. In some ways I think it hurt her worse because she knew who he was and that it was his own people persecuting him. She also knew how unfairly he was being accused. She loved him with all her heart and wanted to protect him but knew she couldn't. Something bad happened to Daddy because someone chose to do something wrong, but he wasn't singled out and killed because he was hated, like Jesus was."

McKenna's eyes quickly brightened as she changed her thought pattern. "I wonder what Santa is going to have us do tonight."

"I don't know, but I do know that if we don't get going and get everything accomplished we need to get done today, we'll have less time to enjoy this evening. Shall we go?"

McKenna jumped off the bed, calling over her shoulder as she headed out the door, "Okay, but I get to wake up the boys this morning!"

A few moments later Emma smiled as she heard the boys' pretentious grumpy attitudes turn into laughter along with McKenna's childish giggles. She pulled the edges of her comforter up and smoothed out the creases on her bed while humming the tune to "Oh Holy Night"—William's favorite carol. Emma stopped short and touched her throat. She could almost hear William's slightly off-key baritone voice humming along with her.

Rather than stop humming and run from any potential emotional pain, she enjoyed the moment and smiled, feeling as if, for a very brief wrinkle in time, he was truly not very far off.

Later that evening as Emma and her family sat down to read the next Santa letter, there was a peace she had not felt in quite a long time. She listened to the words and pondered the meaning contained therein as Jesse read them.

Jensen Family,

Your lives are filled with traditions, and even though you may not realize it, these traditions are the essence of your beliefs and actions.

A tradition is the handing down of stories, beliefs, and customs from generation to generation. Traditions can also be religious, as in the case of Christ's teaching his disciples and the people his Heavenly Father's laws. He taught truth and the order of things as they are in heaven and how they should be here upon this earth. He also taught that if we follow these traditions, or laws, we can return to live in celestial glory once more.

God's laws are ones of order, which means that there are certain ways of doing things. For example, your religious services are filled with traditions that have been passed down from Jesus' teachings through his disciples and prophets from generation to generation. Symbols, services, songs, sacraments—they have all withstood the test of time.

Christmas is also filled with many of these things. What do I represent? What does a tree represent? A wreath? A bow? A candy cane? Why do you give presents? The answer to each of these questions is a part of traditions that savor and celebrate a Savior's birth and what he means to humanity.

Tonight you will participate in one of your family's favorite traditions—decorating a tree with the special ornaments that represent your fondest memories. Here is the means to get a tree and some ornaments for you to add to your collection.

I also want you to take a walk down memory lane as you place your ornaments on the tree. Which are your favorites? I then have a story for you to read by the light of the fire called "A Strange Visitor." It's about some of your other favorite Christmas traditions.

All of these are traditions that have been handed down from generation to generation in your own families. They connect you to the past while grounding you in the present. Hopefully you will find them important enough to carry forward to the next generation.

I love you, which is why I want you to celebrate traditions this night.

Loving always,
Santa

Every year, they had decorated two trees. One was adorned with Emma's fancy coordinated ornaments, gold bows, and white twinkle lights, while the other was filled with colorful lights and ornaments, each representing a memory from a previous year for each member of the family. There were ornaments from when they'd visited the North Pole in Colorado and the year they went to Disneyland the first time, one commemorating the year Jaden first started playing hockey, and then there was the golden sailboat that William had given Emma last year, promising that they'd sail off happily into the sunset once all the kids were raised.

Emma had been able to use money as the issue to avoid the tradition this year, and she was glad that her money woes could help her avoid an uncomfortable situation. The truth, however, was that she did not know if she could bear the thought of dragging all of those precious ornaments out and facing every tender memory. The result would likely be a whole new flood of tears.

But she had no excuses now.

Feeling a bit of boldness rising from inside, she asked Michael to open the box so she could determine what was in store for them. Michael cocked an eyebrow in Emma's direction and, with another confirming nod from her, pulled out an envelope that had a gift certificate for a tree from the closest tree lot, a typed story titled "A Strange Visitor," and some hand-painted ornaments depicting each one of their talents.

Jesse's was a set of books. Besides being so studious, he shared his father's love of reading. Michael's was a car, since he loved anything having to do with the automotive industry. Jaden's ornament was a pair of miniature ice hockey skates representing his passion, and McKenna's was a soccer ball, since she loved playing on her Pink Panther team. Through the process of elimination, Michael figured that Emma's must be the golden heart. William used to kid her about being the heart of their home and that it must be made of gold in order to allow her to put up with such a rowdy bunch. Michael stopped short of pulling out the last ornament, afraid that his mother's strong resolve would dissipate. McKenna, on the other hand, took his hesitation as an invitation and pulled out the last ornament, handing it to her mom.

"Look, Mama. It's Daddy's ornament." Emma took the glass angel and held it ever so carefully. When a rising panic threatened to overcome her, she willfully steeled her shaky determination, stood up, went to the living room, and placed it on her coordinated tree. She was still trying so hard not to give in to the sobs rising from her chest when she noticed something interesting—the angel was reflecting the faces of her children standing behind her. As she looked a little closer, she could see William's features magnified in each one of their faces. She also noticed that they were all looking at her, wondering if this task would prove too great for her.

Those looks made her resolution complete. She squared her shoulders, determined not to disappoint them, and lifted her chin before turning to hug her children. "Let's go get us a Christmas tree."

As he watched the scene unfolding in Emma's living room, hidden by the big pine tree across the street, he couldn't help but smile. All was going according to plan, and from what he'd seen of Emma's reactions, she seemed to be letting at least enough of her sorrow go that she was finally able to remember some of the cherished times. That's all he'd wanted for her—to help her remember how much he'd been blessed even though fate had dealt her some unwelcome blows. But life was like that. Just when you thought you had it all together, life had a way of throwing you a curve ball that would knock even the most sure-footed off balance.

"I guess that's why I always say the only difference between a lump of coal and a diamond is the heat and pressure it can take," he sighed.

It was starting to snow again and, as a few snowflakes slid down the back collar of his worn red flannel coat, chilling his neck, his reverie was broken. He shivered, thinking it was high time he'd better be getting on home. He pulled his fedora a little lower over his brow and sauntered off in the direction with the least amount of light. Tomorrow began the weekend, and he had a lot of preparations to complete.

The Jensens bundled up and headed to Mack's Tree Lot, where they could pick out the perfect tree to decorate with their memories. Emma handed the attending young man her gift certificate. He looked at it for a moment before shaking her hand and grinning. "Oh, so you're the one I'm supposed to help. Let me show you which section to choose from. It's right this way—any of the trees with green tags."

"Wait a minute. How do you know that I'm the one you're supposed to help?" Emma's children listened intently to his answer—that is, except for McKenna, who was off wandering amongst the green-tagged trees.

"Because the old guy described you and your family perfectly. He's also a great tipper! Gave me a thermos of hot chocolate, a hot pizza, and a twenty to make sure I helped you get what you needed and got it tied to the top of your car securely."

"Mama! I found it. I found our perfect tree," squealed McKenna from the other side of the lot.

"Hold on, sweetie."

The boys began battering the young man with questions. "Did you know this man? Did you recognize him at all?" fired Jesse.

"Uhh, no," he replied, somewhat taken aback by their sudden interest.

"How old was he? What did he look like, and what was he wearing?" demanded Michael and Jaden.

"Well . . . he was about sixty to seventy-ish, I think. He was a little round in the belly and about so high," he said as he held his hand out as a marker, "and he was wearing a red coat and a hat."

They all looked at Emma quizzically, except for McKenna, who'd returned to her family's side since they apparently were in no rush to stake a claim on her perfect tree. Overhearing the young man's comments, she began jumping up and down rather enthusiastically.

"It *was* him, Mama, see? It *was* him! I knew it was Santa."

"I must admit," said the young man, finally catching on, "he was a rather jolly sorta guy." Without another word, he turned and headed into the temporary urban pine forest to help the family with McKenna's selection.

The car had barely rolled to a stop when Jesse jumped out to retrieve the tree stand. Michael, close on his heels, climbed into the attic to get their special box of ornaments. Once the tree was secure in the stand with ample water and the skirt placed around its base, Emma and the kids read their story by the light of the family room fireplace before retiring to bed. It'd been a long day, and with tomorrow being Saturday, Emma figured they could afford to let the decorations go for another night.

Once the kids had headed upstairs, Emma stopped by the tree, where she had placed William's new ornaments. She gently plucked it off the branch and gave it a kiss. "Good night, my love. Thank you for watching over us."

The next morning Emma woke to the smell of pancakes and maple syrup. It had been a while since she'd roused herself on a Saturday morning seduced by those familiar scents. William, having been an early riser, had always gotten up on Saturday mornings to bake up a mess (and Emma did mean a mess) of his "Willie-Special Flapjacks" for the family and any guest that might show up. For a brief moment, Emma had been transported back in time and grew excited as she headed downstairs to place a big sloppy kiss on William's cheek and chase away the winter chill by wrapping herself in his arms.

And then she remembered.

Having been harshly brought back to reality, Emma figured that her sons—not William—must've decided that today was a good day to reinstate the tradition. Although Emma's heart now ached with loneliness and longing, she refused to be so consumed with those emotions that she'd end up ruining this day for them. She turned, fetched her bathrobe, and headed downstairs.

"Hey, Mom," greeted Michael. "We figured that since we have so much to do today, we'd better get a good breakfast."

Emma smiled and had barely taken over flipping the pancakes when the doorbell rang. They all—except Emma, who was a bit slow in pace this morning—raced to the door.

No one was there, but in their mysterious benefactor's stead on the doorstep was their Christmas box and another letter. Fortunately for the man in the red coat, they were still barefoot and in their pajamas and couldn't wander after him too far. And that is exactly what he had counted on as he followed the trail between houses before ringing the doorbell and running back the way he'd come. When he was safely a couple of houses away, he stopped to try and catch his breath. Bent over, he laughed to himself—not at his good fortune at having succeeded in remaining anonymous, but because he was having such a darn good time! "I haven't had this much fun, or been this out of breath, since I was a kid playing night games in Green Park," he mused.

After checking to make sure the coast was clear and having gotten his heart rate back to a normal level, he backtracked through the neighborhood and slid into his old Jeep Wagoneer. He still had to finish his preparations for the next few days.

They all took note that if they were to ever capture their "Santa," they'd have to start wearing running shoes at all times. Since a cursory scan of their surroundings ferreted out no signs of a visitor, they picked up the box after another quick glance and brought it inside. Emma had them gather around the table so she could continue cooking while Michael read the newest letter.

Jensen Family,

Laughter is important. Humor is nature's salve to soothe an aching soul. Parents will go to almost any length—including making a fool of themselves—to hear their child's laughter.

A baby's laugh is music to the ears, but, unfortunately, as we get older, we many times lose the pure joy that our Heavenly Father wants us to recognize and feel. The ugliness of the world jades us, and that joyous spirit which invites that childlike laughter is harder to capture.

Ecclesiastes 3 tells us that to every thing there is a season and a purpose under the sun. Just as there is a time to be born and a time to die, a time to plant and a time to harvest, there is also a time to weep and a time to laugh, a time to mourn and a time to dance.

Even the Savior understood the importance of laughter as he took his disciples and administered to his sheep on the Sabbath, saying, "Blessed be ye poor: for yours is the Kingdom of God. Blessed are ye that hunger now: for ye shall be filled. Blessed are ye that weep now: for ye shall laugh. Blessed are ye when men shall hate you, and when they shall separate you from their company, and shall reproach you and cast out your name as evil for the son of man's sake. Rejoice ye in that day, and leap for joy: for behold, your reward is great in heaven" (Luke 6:20–23).

As much as it pains me, you have learned well the meaning of these words. But just as you have seen great aching sorrow, true inexpressible joy is waiting for you, for you cannot have one without having first experienced the other.

Jensens, I love you and have known of your pain, which is why tonight I want you to laugh and know that good times are ahead. I have sent some of your favorite things to watch and listen to, along with some treats. Take a moment afterward to talk about your funniest memories and laugh! Connect with good feelings this night.

Loving always,

Santa

Inside the box were a few comedy routines done by their favorite comedians on CD, some favorite comedies on DVD, a box of popcorn, and a six-pack of root beer.

Emma laughed as she picked up the case to *National Lampoon's Christmas Vacation*. Only William—and apparently their new friend—could have known that something so purely simple and ridiculous would be just the thing to cap off this day and the previous week. Emma figured they might as well enjoy every minute of it, so after cleaning up the breakfast dishes, they all stayed in their pajamas and decorated the tree while listening to one of their new Christmas CDs.

Emma's sides felt bruised from laughing so hard and for so long the day before. Tears had run down her cheeks and not because she was sad, but because she and the kids had been overcome by chuckles, which turned into hoots and then wild guffaws at Clark Griswold and his wacky family.

It had felt good to laugh again. Laughter had become a rarity since she'd buried William, but today was another day, and she realized as she looked at the clock on her nightstand, church would be starting in a little over an hour.

After showering and styling her hair, Emma smiled into the mirror before looking toward William's closet. She rummaged through his top shelf as she looked for the cymbal-playing monkey he'd given her a couple of years back on Valentine's Day. Still basking in the good feelings of last night's hilarity, she walked to each of the boys' rooms and set the chimp next to them before flipping on the switch and stepping back a few feet.

The responses varied from Jesse screaming and flinging the monkey across the room to Jaden sleepily rolling over to repeatedly bat at his alarm clock to quiet the offending sound with no success. Michael's eyes had flown open immediately as he was confronted with the noisy animal sitting next to him, trying to decipher if he was dreaming or in some kind of odd reality. He figured it out rather quickly though, as he caught a glimpse of his mother giggling like a giddy child.

"I haven't seen you act like that since Dad finished the taxes two years ago and told you that we were getting almost eight thousand back. It's good to see you laugh," said Michael, having come out of his groggy stupor.

McKenna hadn't been woken up in such a spirited way since she was already stumbling out of her room as Emma and Michael exited his. Her slumber had been rudely interrupted when Jaden, still batting at his alarm, had knocked it off his dresser onto his head and howled at the injustice of some mornings.

Emma clapped. "Okay, kids, now that I've had my fun, it's time to get ready for church. We leave in exactly one hour."

Emma was beginning to realize that she'd somehow managed to let grief devour her to the point of being an almost unrecognizable shell. As she walked down the halls at church, she'd been nearly overwhelmed at how many people had given her various compliments like, "It's so nice to see you smiling," and "There's something different about you. I can't put my finger on it, but the change is good—you've never looked better."

She'd been so consumed with sadness and loss that, between the two emotions, she had scarcely remembered how to live. Somewhere in the deep recesses of her mind, Emma had figured that if she found happiness in this world without William, it would in some way be a betrayal to him. But their children needed a mother—someone to guide them through their early years, and since William couldn't (at least in a physical way), she'd have to be the one stepping up to the plate. Emma was sure that if William presently had any say in the matter, he'd want his four children growing up with good things like laughter, appreciation, love, beauty, knowledge that the world was a good place, and—for those times when it wasn't—a sense of peace until understanding came.

Emma had barely pulled the car into the driveway when the car doors flew open and the kids all jumped out. Irritated because she hadn't come to a complete stop yet, she was about to reprimand them for their reckless behavior when she noticed the cause of their excitement. There on the front step was their Christmas box and another full sack accompanied by another Santa letter. Emma, having just been bitten by the excitement bug herself, stepped on the gas and quickly parked the car.

She'd barely set foot in the living room when Jaden, taking her presence as the go ahead, ripped into the envelope and read its contents.

Jensen Family,

Friendship is the icing on life's cake—that little extra that makes it so delicious! Everyone has a family, but to have been blessed with friends is truly a divine honor!

There is an old adage that says, "Our lives are filled with many joys and blessings without end, but one of the greatest joys in life is to have or be a friend."

Think of the hardest times in life. Besides family, who has stood there beside you cheering you on, encouraging you, and lending support? Family is given to you by birth, but your friends here on earth are your family by choice.

No one was a better friend to those who needed a listening ear, a shoulder to cry upon, or help in any form than Christ himself. He cried with Mary and Martha when they mourned their brother's death, even though he knew within moments they'd be rejoicing the miracle of life as it was breathed back into his body. He wept because he was a true friend who grieved as they grieved, cried because they cried, and then gave them back their brother and rejoiced because they rejoiced.

This is a true friend—someone who loves you through your imperfections, helps you carry your burdens, ministers to your broken heart, laughs at your lame jokes, is proud when you succeed, and pushes you to be a better person just by having known them.

This year as you have faced many trials, besides your faith, it's your friends who have gotten you through. They have walked the paths with you, shielded you, protected you, and loved you. Tonight you will have the opportunity to thank them and return the favors.

You have each been given a small friendship bear and a note card. I want you to take these and, with someone in mind who needs a boost, write a special message to leave with the bear anonymously on their doorstep so they may think that *any one of a hundred friends could be watching over them.*

You will also deliver your gifts to your neighborhood friends, for they are the ones who have made living here on earth and in this neighborhood such a joy.

Jensens, I love you, which is why tonight I want you to remember exactly what friendship has meant to you and count your blessings in terms of your many friends.

Loving always,
Santa

The box was filled to the brim with the five friendship bears along with some embossed note cards to write messages of love and concern and some of the supplies to make holiday survival kits. The bag contained the rest.

My goodness, Emma thought to herself, *Santa's left enough for all our friends this year and plenty for those the next decade to come!*

Michael ran to get a pad of paper and their neighborhood contact list, school directories, and his mother's address book. After an hour and a half of compiling lists, Emma changed her mind on their survival kit stock and began to wonder if they'd have enough to give something to everyone who'd blessed their lives over the course of the last year.

"Come on, kids," Emma said as she picked up the heavy box and carried it to the kitchen table. "It looks like we have a lot of work to do."

Jesse typed up the tags while Michael cut up the ribbons to tie the cellophane bags. Jaden and McKenna dumped all the treats into bowls while Emma made some quick sandwiches.

Once they'd eaten and finished assembling the kits, each family member chose a special person as the recipient for their friendship bear and wrote an anonymous message to deliver along with the gift. Jesse chose a single mom whose only son had just gotten married, and Jaden and Michael chose friends who were struggling. McKenna chose her grandparents because they too missed her daddy. She figured that William would want "his special little girl" to include Papa and Nana in the Christmas he and Santa were sharing with them.

After careful consideration, Emma chose William's best friend, Paul, who was more like a brother than a friend. They'd grown up together, gone to school together, double dated together, and raised their families together. Had it not been for Paul, who had begun dating and seriously falling for Emma's roommate Marianne, she and William would probably never have met. It was Paul and Marianne who had helped Emma get through the funeral arrangements and find a stable job. Emma was sure that if there was a person out there, other than William's parents, who mourned as ferociously as herself, it was Paul.

After delivering almost all the gifts, their focus turned to the last five—the friendship bears. Emma parked the car down the street from each recipient's house so the giver could set their gift on the porch, ring the doorbell, and run. Jaden, getting a real kick out of this activity, graciously offered to deliver Emma's for her.

When they got to their grandparents' home, Emma parked around the corner as Jaden and McKenna sneaked up to their front porch. Emma and the other two boys watched, making sure they were well hidden in the shadows. She smiled when, after they'd they pounded on the front door, Jaden grabbed McKenna's hand and took off running with his little sister flying behind him like an erratic kite. Once they'd safely jumped into the car, Emma started the engine and pulled away before turning on the lights to finish driving back to their own home.

When he heard the door chimes, Walter jumped out of his chair and scurried to the entryway. He opened the door and found on his stoop a small flannel bear sitting on a lovely white embossed note card. He picked them up, looked around, and smiled as he watched the tail ends of his grandchildren dive behind a bush and into a car parked around the corner. Still grinning, he returned to the TV room.

"Well, Mother, it looks as if we've had some visitors." He chuckled as he handed her the bear and picked up his reading glasses so he could read the childish scrawl.

A hart is red, the skie is blue.

Evin tho yor son is gon, he is stil ner to you.

Hevin isint that far awae. Sumbudy lovs you varee much and wants you to be hapy. XOXOXO

Emma rose early. She needed to get a few extra things done so she'd have time tonight to do their Santa activity after Jaden's game. But before she started on her list of chores, the more childish part of her took over with a hankering to sneak downstairs and peek out the door. She was determined to find a clue, any clue at all, as to who might be visiting them. Instead, she found the Christmas box with its accompanying letter several hours early, right in its place upon their doorstep.

As she opened the door, she heard Jesse's deep, gravely voice. "Hey, what're you doin'?"

"Okay, you caught me. I wanted to see if I could figure out who the mystery guy is, but he beat me to the punch and delivered everything early."

"Who says it has to be a guy?" Jesse inquired, looking at

her with a cocked eyebrow while speculating as to her real purpose for being on the doorstep this early in the morning.

"What? Oh, you mean . . . no! No, it's not me, really! I honestly just wanted to see if I could find some sort of clue while I had the time and silence to think about it."

"Whatever you say, Mom," Jesse half-believingly countered as he headed off to shower. Emma looked back out the door one last time to search around but found nothing. She placed the items by the tree and then headed back upstairs.

After Emma had been thoroughly interrogated by Jesse, and the family had hurriedly eaten breakfast and cleaned up, they stole a few moments so they could go in by the tree before finishing getting ready for school. They were all a bit curious as to why their Santa letter and box had arrived so early—that is, except for Jesse, who was still looking at his mother, smugly thinking he knew the answer to that question.

Jensen Family,

Not a one of us could make it through life obtaining our goals without the support of others. Just as a table needs legs, we need those around us to keep us steady.

Many times in the scriptures, the Savior makes reference to his Father in Heaven, saying that they are of one mind. Their purposes were singular, their goals were the same, and all their actions worked toward these means.

Tonight I want you to ponder the gift of a family's support.

Jesse, you are one who has always taken your studies so seriously, but test taking has always been your nemesis. Capturing the knowledge you've studied and putting it to paper is what stresses you out to the point of freezing. With your mother's help, this study and quiz program can help you conquer any test phobias before you hit the college path. You have a good mind, and with a little bit of instruction, your tests will begin to show just how good it is! Test anxiety will no longer be a problem for you.

Michael, in this box is an apron and two books—one on cooking techniques and another full of great camping recipes. Besides your love for the automotive industry, your love of anything culinary makes you the favorite camp chef in your scout troop and has also been a huge help to your mother, who has more than willingly turned her kitchen over to you. Since her time has become so limited in the last year, you are the one who has used your talent and love for cooking to help her where others could not. Keep enhancing this talent and you will be able to add spice to many people's lives.

Jaden, tonight your family will support you in one of your great passions as you play a game you love. They will be cheering for you, proud to claim you as one of their own as you once again lead your team on the ice. Since your love is hockey, in this box you will find a bungee ball that will help you with your hand-eye coordination as you train to be the best goalie you can be. You will also find a couple of packs of NHL cards so that you can add them to your collection of dreams.

McKenna, you are growing big and strong, and you help your soccer team out by running fast like a cheetah. In this box are some special vitamins that will help you stay healthy while growing even bigger and stronger, so you can continue to learn and develop. I have also placed in the box one of my favorite Christmas books to read with your mom and brothers, since I know you are becoming such a good reader.

Emma, you have sons who have helped you out when you needed it financially, mentally, and physically. They are examples to you of understanding, faith, and hard work. You also have a little girl who has been a ray of sunshine on even the most dreary of days. I can give you nothing more than what God has already given you with these four wonderful children. Enjoy them this season.

Jensens, I love you, which is why tonight I want you to celebrate the support of a good family who will help you reach your goals.

Loving always,
Santa

While Jesse was pretty sure he understood why their Santa activities corresponded so well with their schedules, Emma was feeling tinges of uneasiness because someone apparently knew their lives awfully well. Consciously pushing back feelings of agitation and replacing them with a hurried sense of responsibility, Emma gave each child a schedule and a list of tasks to do before they all hurried off in separate directions.

After everyone had returned home that evening, they piled into the car so they could go support Jaden in his game. Not only did they enjoy the competition, but Emma particularly enjoyed seeing so many of the friends who had supported them throughout the past year. They had warmly embraced their family, acting as if the Jensens had never been forced to abandon their spots in the stands, and although

William's loud cheering voice was certainly missed, the rest of the team's families were glad to have Emma and the kids back among them.

After arriving home that night, and with all the kids off to bed, Emma curled up with her patchwork quilt in the living room and once again stared out the front window. It was snowing again. It wasn't that long ago that she had looked into the darkness and seen nothing but a dark, cold future. But having recently been lured back to the land of the living, she'd begun to once again see a few snatches of hope and feel twinges of peace intermingled with sprinklings of joy. What had once been a nightly ritual of sitting in the darkness crying while curled up in her blanket had turned into evenings of anticipation with her children.

"William," she whispered into the night, "I didn't believe it was possible to ever enjoy Christmas without you, but somehow, someway, life has seemed almost bearable pretending that you're not so far away."

She smiled, and instead of an irrational instinct drawing her toward keeping a cold grave warm, she wrapped her quilt a little tighter around herself, content to imagine William's loving arms as they caressed her as softly as a warm summer breeze.

He watched from behind the archway and smiled with satisfaction. He saw peace in her face, which meant that everything was on track for what needed to be done next. Tomorrow would be tough, but it was a necessary step for this family to heal. Tomorrow's had been the toughest gift for him to put together, and yet, in some ways, he also knew it would be the one that would allow the most progress for them all—including himself. It was the one gift that, if everyone could come to understand and embrace, could heal the entire world.

After such a long year, Emma was finally beginning to regain some emotional balance. She hadn't realized how much she'd been teetering until their mystery visitor had lulled her into living again by showing her how to enjoy her family. She'd woken up rested and refreshed without the heaviness of swollen eyelids and a puffy face from crying herself to sleep. She noticed that her children seemed happier too—as if they were virtual mirrors of how her life was going. Could the clouds that had darkened her days really have affected them so adversely? If so, then maybe it was good that someone had seen fit to pull her out of her melancholy so that her children would have a chance at a somewhat normal and happy life—even if it was impossible for Emma to ever get over missing William terribly. She owed it to her family, she owed it to William, and she owed it to herself.

When Emma returned home that night, the kids had already set the box and the most recent letter in by the tree and were all poised at the kitchen table, ready to dig into dinner. Emma needed only to seat herself and say a prayer. Their evening meals as of late had become more of a necessity before being able to move on to bigger and better things rather than being their time to reconnect as a family. Emma was sure Jaden agreed, which is what had prompted him to fix peanut butter and jelly sandwiches served on paper plates with chips as a side and Oreos for dessert. *At least he's willingly helping out, and I bet he even offers to do the dishes*, she thought to herself.

True to Emma's predictions, Jaden quickly cleared the table, swished a wet rag around in circles on the table's surface, and put the plant back, all while Emma and McKenna swallowed their last few bites. Neither had to ask where he then disappeared to—the whistling from the living room gave him away.

Emma picked McKenna up from her chair and followed after him while McKenna licked the last of the jelly from her fingers. As they all sat down, Emma nodded to Michael to read their next Santa letter.

Jensen family,

This has been a year full of challenges as you have come to understand the concepts of justice, mercy, and forgiveness. These three things are something we all want but have a hard time giving. Why is that?

The Savior's whole purpose in coming to earth was to balance the scales of justice so that we could seek forgiveness and mercy. He was the ultimate example as he saved a woman scorned, saying, "Let him who is without sin cast the first stone." Who at that point could even think about reaching for a rock to throw in her direction? Yet today we still want to judge, forgetting that we have not earned the right to do so by giving an innocent life and allowing innocent blood to be shed for those who've trespassed against God and their fellowmen. Only one person ever earned that right, and he did so freely so that we all could have the opportunity to return to heaven.

Through his mercy we have justice, for those who trespass against us—if they do not seek repentance in this life—will have the debt to pay and the suffering to bear in the next. Therefore, justice cannot be dethroned by mercy. For those who have repented, the scales are balanced and the debt has already been paid. We then have the blessing of forgiveness, and it is a sure fact that repentance followed by his forgiveness makes the most brilliant day of the darkest night.

But to seek his forgiveness one must also forgive. And it is not for their own sake or own personal compensation but as an acknowledgment and acceptance that what has been done for one has also been done for another, even if that other has grievously trespassed against you, remembering that we are all God's children. You can read in Matthew 18 how this concept was taught by our Savior in the parable of the unmerciful servant. It is a masterfully designed lesson on the meaning of the simple words in the Lord's Prayer: "Forgive us our debts as we forgive our debtors."

Tonight you will celebrate these gifts so generously offered by Christ. In this box are the items that will allow you to remember the justice that has already been served, and a few more things that will help you to find mercy in your hearts and then hopefully have the ability to forgive.

I love you, which is why tonight I want you to experience justice, mercy, and forgiveness.

Loving always,
Santa

Emma stared straight ahead as a quelling feeling of unease made her wonder for the first time during this process if she could do what was required of her or if she should get up and run before she could be dragged into a nightmare. Justice she could handle, but mercy and forgiveness were quite another thing. To accomplish that would mean that she'd have to accept what had been done and come to peace with it somehow. But how could she ever possibly do that, knowing she'd been left without her best friend and her children had been left without their father? To be merciful and forgive, to Emma's current way of thinking, would be the same as lessening her husband's life . . . wouldn't it? Was it possible to mourn him and still forgive?

Watching the tears well up in their mother's eyes, the two older boys sat in silence, not knowing what to say or do. McKenna was still too busy licking her fingers to understand what had just transpired. Jaden, however, who was never at a loss for words and lacked a certain social panache, blurted out, "Well, time's a wastin'. Let's get this party started" before diving toward the box and throwing aside the lid.

Jesse didn't know whether to smack his younger brother or follow his own curiosity. But as a look of confusion spread across Jaden's face, Jesse decided that curiosity would win out and quickly got down off the couch so he could see the box's contents.

He too was now confused.

Michael and McKenna, looking at their brothers' faces, now had to see for themselves what was in the box. Only Emma kept her seat, afraid that if she moved, she might lose whatever decorum of stability she had maintained while she processed her swirling thoughts.

"Is that . . . him?" Jaden asked incredulously, staring at the photo on top of the clippings, pictures, an envelope, and a book.

Jesse picked it up, remembering the hard dark eyes he'd watched in court as he'd looked for anything—anything at all—that would explain why their lives had had to cross this miserable man's. But the man had stared straight ahead, acting as if their family's presence was of little importance to him—as if they were a nuisance, a blip, or an insignificant detail in his encumbered day.

Emma took the picture, also remembering those eyes, but this picture showed the man with a smile, a genuine smile that radiated upward to those dark orbs. Guillermo Menendez looked happy. This likeness of him, although Emma instinctively knew it was the same man she'd seen in court, didn't look at all like him. What, she wondered, had happened?

Emma turned to the box and pulled out another picture

of a young boy with his mother and a scruffy looking dog. With a bright sun shining in the background, glistening off what appeared to be an old tin silo keeping watch over lush green fields, the mother stood among the plants, looking at her son with adoration. Her perfectly white teeth made up a smile as radiant as the man's in the first photo. The small boy looked straight ahead at whoever was capturing the moment, with one hand protecting his eyes from the glare of the sun while waving with the other. The dog was sitting on his hind legs, head cocked to one side, also looking at the person behind the camera.

Emma turned the picture over to read the shaky scrawl, "Guillermo, el perro Cabra, y Mamá."

"Look at this one," said Jesse as he handed another picture to his mother. It was of a sad little boy standing by an elongated pine box with a few wildflowers scattered on top. Every picture they looked at was of a crucial scene in Guillermo's life, a scene that had helped shape and mold him into the man he was today.

Under the pictures were several newspaper clippings that together created a time line Emma found hard to relive. Like those who gawk at the macabre although the scene promises to pull tears and silent screams, Emma's strange fascination made her want to understand the meaning of all this, and so she garnered every bit of courage she had in order to continue on. She picked up the first newspaper clipping and read:

> William Jensen, 42, of South Point was killed in a hit and run accident on December 24, 2005, as he was walking back to his car after leaving the Midtown Shopping Center. He was crossing South Central when he was hit and killed by Guillermo Emil Menendez, 34, who according to bystanders, slowed almost to a stop before accelerating rapidly and slamming into Jensen. Menendez sped off but was later caught by police in Midvalley.
>
> "We're not sure if his actions were intentional or not, but we intend to find out during the process of our investigation," said South Point Police Chief Victor Higgins.
>
> Besides the question of intent, sources at the police department also state that alcohol was a definite factor. Breathalyzer tests taken that night calculated a blood alcohol level of .17—almost two times the legal limit for driving impaired in this state.
>
> Menendez is being held in the Fairfax County Jail without bail while he awaits a court hearing scheduled for later this week. Jensen leaves behind a wife, three sons, and a daughter.

Emma's eyes welled up with tears again as she looked at the black-and-white photo of the crime scene with an overlay of Menendez's mug shot. Michael moved over and put his arm around his mother.

The rest of the newspaper clips were about the investigation, trial, and sentencing until they abruptly came to a stop—just like her sweet William's life had—as the media moved on to another day, another story.

After twenty years of marriage, William had decided to surprise Emma with a custom-made necklace for Christmas. On Christmas Eve, he'd gotten the call that the stones—a birthstone for each member of their family—had been securely placed into the heart setting and the project was finally completed. When the jeweler found out why William never made it to his shop, he had sent the completed project to Emma free of charge. But looking at that sixth stone, William's birthstone, she hadn't yet had the heart to wear it.

"Mom, you should read this," said Jesse as he handed her a book marked with a red ribbon. Emma opened the Bible and read the highlighted passage. "Blessed are the merciful: for they shall obtain mercy" (Matthew 5:7).

The next item to come out of the box was a tape. As

Jaden rushed off to fetch his portable stereo, Emma wrestled with her emotions, wondering if she really wanted to hear what was on it. She'd done well thus far to keep from sobbing in front of her children but was admittedly very close to being pushed over the edge.

But when Jaden returned, with nary a thought toward Emma's unspoken thoughts, he popped in the tape and pressed play. In faltering English, a woman introduced herself as Belin Gabriella Cortez—Guillermo's older sister.

Before Emma could reach over and press the stop button, the woman's sad voice asked for the chance to explain. Something in Emma—maybe curiosity or maybe the need for understanding—made her sit back down.

"I know how my brother has hurt your family in ways we can never repay, but it is my desire to tell you about him so you can hopefully understand that he is not a monster but simply a man who did a monstrous thing—a thing for which he will spend the rest of his days being punished by rather than for.

"You can see in the pictures that when Guillermo was a little boy, he was happy and had all the promise of a bright future. We all did. Guillermo would run and play in the fields by our hacienda with his dog, Cabra. When Guillermo first got Cabra, he'd help Papa by taking the goats to the nearby field and try to train Cabra to watch over them. But that silly dog thought it too was a goat and would eat the grass and grains right along the side of them. That's how he came by his name, Cabra, which means 'goat.'

"Those were good times, the times before Guillermo came home from school and found Mama lying dead in the kitchen with balls of dough around her and a tortilla singed to ashes in the heavy iron skillet.

"She had surprised the *ladrones*—thieves—by being home since they had mistaken me, as I left for school, for her. Papa and I returned later that day and found Guillermo encircling Mama's chest with his own small body, sobbing inconsolably as his tears drenched her blouse and mingled with the blood soaking her hair."

Emma stared at the picture taken in the field and in her mind's eye painted a picture of that little boy as grief wracked his small frame and anguish bit him deeply, refusing to relinquish its tightening grip on his small heart. She knew that feeling. It was the one that had urged her—if even for a brief insane moment—to think about jumping in on William's coffin before it could be covered with even one shovelful of dirt. As Emma had stood in solidarity by his grave site, keeping with a serene widow's appearance, her mind obsessed with how she could keep the earth from swallowing him up. Emma was sure that each layer of dirt separating her from William might as well be an eternity, and if she could just prevent the soil from obstructing her view of the box that housed his body, maybe he wouldn't seem so far off. It was that same instinct that in moments of irrational thought led her physically and sometimes just mentally to his grave, wanting to cover it with a quilt as thoughts of warming his body and taking care of him warmed her soul.

After a year though, Emma was finally beginning to realize that it wasn't about keeping William warm as much as it was about keeping him close.

Guillermo's sister continued on with her tale as she narrated his dismal life. Guillermo's father, unable to deal with his own grief from losing his wife, had immersed himself into a drunken stupor, keeping his heart well medicated and unable to feel the pain he was sure he could not endure. Losing much of what they'd worked so hard for and feeling like he was drowning on the land that held so many memories, their father had eventually taken both of his children to the United States, leaving behind all they'd known for a chance to start over. But even if grief had finally relinquished its grip on their father's will to move on, years of alcohol abuse did not, and he died three weeks after Guillermo's fourteenth birthday. That is when his older sister and her new husband had taken Guillermo in to their already crowded apartment.

"My brother tried to adapt, but he never quite felt like he had a place where he could find peace," Belin continued. "He ran away several times and was becoming hardened on the streets when he met Maria, a young girl who saw something good in his heart. When Guillermo was twenty-three, he and Maria married.

"For eight years they tried to start a family but had no success. They finally gave up, but in their tenth year of marriage, Maria found out she was expecting. The prospects of having his own family put Guillermo on cloud nine. I've never seen two happier people as they anxiously looked forward to the birth of their daughter. On the night Maria went into labor, Guillermo strapped her carefully into the car and headed to West Valley Medical. A block away from the hospital, a man on a cell phone who was trying to write down directions didn't see the light turn red and crashed into the passenger side of Guillermo's car as he was turning left. Maria's uterus was ruptured and neither hers nor the baby's life could be saved.

"As Guillermo's wife lay there bleeding, the man stood motionless, staring off into some unseen world with glazed-over eyes while mumbling about the business deal that might be lost and the higher insurance premiums for his BMW that were now sure to come. Guillermo only remembers seeing the man's face, so consumed with his own life that he wouldn't lend a hand to help another. Whether it was shock or complete self-centeredness, we'll never know—the outcome would still have been the same. Whatever emotion it was that held him captive that night had refused to let him see beyond his own encapsulated realm while Maria bled to death. He never even lifted a finger to help, offer aid, or seek assistance. A stranger who had witnessed the accident finally took charge and called for an ambulance."

Belin continued with Guillermo's story of anguished decline as he fought the hatred and other raw emotions that sought to destroy him. On the night of William's death, Guillermo invited alcohol, which he'd always seen as an enemy, to drown out his sorrows as he remembered how his father had drunk himself into stupors until he passed out for days at a time, unable to think or feel. Surely,

Guillermo surmised, that kind of living death couldn't be any worse than the excruciating ache that kept him up at night and haunted his days. Leaving work early, he headed for a bar downtown where he could be alone and drink until his fuzzy head and dulled senses falsely allowed him to welcome his mattress and a peaceful slumber rather than cringe at the nightmares sure to come.

He'd gone only a few blocks when he spotted a man walking jauntily across the street. That face—it was blurry—but so familiar . . . it must be him! Rage bubbled within Guillermo as he remembered the man's insensitivity and the injustice that had followed.

Since the laws at the time of the accident defined cell phone usage as a distraction—equal to that of changing the music station or eating—no criminal indictment had ever been filed. The man had been cited and forced to pay a hefty fee and take driver awareness classes, but he'd never taken legal or financial responsibility for the death of Guillermo's wife and unborn child. And since there had been no extenuating circumstances like prior infractions, a sketchy driving record, or the involvement of alcohol or any other controlled substances, the accident had been classified as just that—an accident caused by a distracted driver.

While trying to avoid being crushed by his grief, Guillermo had been forced, with the help of the few family and friends he had, to deal with the financial repercussions of someone else's choices as he scraped enough money together to give Maria and his daughter a proper Christian burial. And without as much as an apology, any tokens of compassion, or understanding for Guillermo's anguish, or even an acknowledgment of wrong-doing on behalf of the man, the unfairness of the whole situation had become like acid being poured into Guillermo's festering wounds. He hated this world—this world that was filled with so much injustice for those who try to live a good life.

But here, Guillermo had calculated, was his chance. Justice had equaled the scales and placed the man whose countenance haunted his memories and had ruined his life right in front of him. If only he could see the man's face clearly and watch that look of terror knowing that he, for a moment at least, was experiencing the same kind of pain and harsh realization of mortality that Maria had felt while Guillermo cradled her in his arms until her last breath escaped her lips.

Rational thought completely escaped Guillermo as seething hatred and lust for revenge consumed him, becoming a hunger not to be denied. As if in a long-awaited dream, he pressed his foot to the gas pedal, making the tires screech as they surged forward. Guillermo did not remember much more than the thud and an instant feeling of panic as he faced the reality of what he'd just done. Not knowing what else to do, he returned home and sat in an old recliner, weeping and shaking uncontrollably while he waited for the police to knock on his door.

Emma stared ahead as tears streamed down her face, making zebra stripes out of her mascara. William's death had been an accident—a case of mistaken identity—not that Guillermo Menendez's thought process could justify what he'd done, but at least Emma understood that William had not been singled out. He'd been at the right place at the right time as a man's lifetime of grief had crashed head on into the present. Emma couldn't help but feel a sense of kinship with the man who'd turned her life upside down. He knew what she felt just as she knew his pain and the nightmares he'd faced.

"Mom?" Michael prodded at her thoughts. "Are you okay? Do you want to go on?"

Emma saw that Michael was holding an envelope, but as her gaze drifted from his hands—so much like his father's—to his face and then to the faces of each of her children. She realized that she didn't know Guillermo Menendez at all, and yet her heart ached for him. He'd never been able to look into the eyes of his own child knowing the culmination of a perfect love as she and William had as they'd ushered each of their children into this world. By having a family, she and William had together created a bridge into the future.

Guillermo had been so close to that kind of joy, but it had all been ripped away from him in an instant. Emma personally couldn't imagine sitting here alone without her children after losing William. They'd given her the strength to go on without William. The fact that Guillermo had managed to survive as long as he had without any physical lifeline to hang on to had been a miracle. No, Emma did not know this man at all.

She looked back at her second son's face. "What is that, Michael?"

"I think it's a letter, and it's addressed to you." He handed it over to Emma. She carefully opened the seal on the wrinkled and smudged envelope and read the words to herself before she allowed Jesse to read it aloud.

I know that I am the last person you would ever want to hear from, but I am writing this so that you can know how sorry I am for being the cause of your pain and loss.

I know that Belin has told you about my life, but I wish she hadn't. There is no excuse for what I have done and the pain I have caused. There is even less of an excuse since I know all too well what loss can do to the soul. I should never have thought, even for a second, that my brand of justice could compensate for what had been taken from me, especially since your husband was an innocent man. My mother used to teach me that all the water in the world will not sink a ship unless it gets inside. I allowed hate and rationalizations to dictate my actions and my life. I allowed all the bad in the world to sink my soul, and now I am punished by my own sins. No prison could ever inflict a heavier or more bitter yoke than that which I've placed upon myself.

Every day I sit upon my bunk and see Maria's eyes full of disappointment for the crimes I have committed. She was too good for me, and I never did deserve her. I think sometimes that God was merciful in taking them away so I could not taint them with the malice, evil, and sorrow that I have thrust upon your family.

After we buried Maria and our child, Belin gave me a hand-stitched square to put on my wall. Oh, how I wish that I had heeded the advice it gave! Instead, I let the injustice of this world *consume my soul until I became that which I most hated. I do not ask for forgiveness—I do not deserve it—but I do not want you to end up a despicable creature like me. Remember the love that was taught, the times you shared, and thank God for the gift of time with someone you loved. And whatever you do, do not go into eternity knowing you have done nothing but disappoint them. Although I believe rotting here for the rest of my days is too good for me, I do not want hatred and anger to rob another life—your life.*

I can never pay you back for what I have done, but I can show you what life is to be if you allow this raging cycle of hurt and despair to consume you as I allowed it to consume me.

Eternally regretful and with a heart full of sorrow,
Guillermo

Jaden pulled one last item out of the box. It was a linen square with delicate hand stitching and a decorative border. It said, "In the very depth of your soul, dig a grave. Let it be as some forgotten spot to which no path leads, and there in the eternal silence bury the wrong which you have suffered. Your heart will feel as if a load has fallen from it, and divine peace will come to abide with you."

After Emma had said good night to each of her children and tucked McKenna into bed, she returned to the living room and stared at the linen square. Before tonight, she'd never thought it possible to forgive what had been done to her family. But now, she didn't see how she couldn't. Just as in Guillermo's visions as he'd faced the disappointment in Maria's eyes, Emma could not help but see William's gentle face encouraging her to forgive and go on living as he would have her and the children do. If they did not, she would only be wasting the love, hopes, and dreams they'd created together, and she could never disappoint William that way. While he would be the eyes from heaven watching over their children when Emma could not, she would be the arms, laughter, tears, and kisses that would get them through their day-to-day lives.

The words in Matthew kept resounding through her thoughts. "Blessed are the merciful, for they shall obtain mercy." She couldn't help but think how ironic it was that the man who'd changed her life forever, and whose name was the same as her husband's in Spanish, had been the one to help her understand the language of a forgiving soul. Guillermo may not feel as if he deserved mercy, but Emma had definitely concluded that she was not the one who needed to be exacting judgment. Only one person had earned the right to do that—the only perfect man who'd ever walked the face of the earth and the one whose birth she and her family were in the middle of celebrating. Emma was beginning to understand the Messiah's true mission. If anyone could mete out the perfect mixture of justice and mercy, it was him. Emma fully believed that the Savior was the only one who knew all the extenuating circumstances in our lives. He could not only heal broken hearts, but level the scales of justice, making sure that those owed were paid and those in debt received relief.

Emma thought again of her children and thanked God for those four wonderful blessings. William lived on. She saw it not only in their features but in how they were living their lives as they turned into good, compassionate, and loving people like their father. No, she didn't have to make life hard for Guillermo Menendez. He'd done that all on his own when he'd abandoned any hope of ever being the man he had one day dreamed of being or of ever having the things that every person should be blessed with—a family, a home, and people who loved him and found value in him.

With all her thoughts still rattling around in her head, Emma perked up and ran to retrieve a few items from her rolltop desk. When she came back to the living room, she set aside her old quilt, picked up her new one, and wrapped it around her shoulders before tucking her feet up, pulling the book off the side table, and beginning to write a letter to Guillermo Menendez.

Fortunately the weather had calmed down or he would've been soaked to the skin by now. Although he'd parked his car close in case he needed the instant comforts of a dry place and a heater to stave off losing any extremities, he'd remained perfectly still as he watched every emotion play out upon her face. He'd known this would be a difficult night and prayed with all his heart that William would forgive him if the desired effect was not the ultimate outcome. William had been such an example of grace under pressure—a useful skill he'd learned when he'd chosen a career in psychiatry and counseling.

He laughed to himself. "And a rather useful trade at that," he mused, remembering the day he and his wife had visited Emma and the children and secretly "borrowed" William's textbook on dealing with grief. After watching every bit of life waste away until there was hardly any sparkle in Emma's usually vibrant eyes, he and his wife had decided that something needed to be done to help her get through this. That's when he'd run across the letters—one for Emma and each of the children—that William had given him over a year ago with the explicit directions to leave them on the doorstep while the family was over celebrating Christmas Eve with some neighborhood friends. When the accident happened, the letters had been forgotten as his mind turned to planning a funeral instead of celebrating the Christmas season.

But as he and his wife had prayed for direction and guidance on how to help Emma, he came across the letters while cleaning behind the bookcase, where they'd slipped the year before. The rest of the plan had come together easily as the letters had given him an idea for a non-threatening and anonymous way to make it a memorable and hopefully happy Christmas for Emma and the kids.

But as is the way with good things and glad tidings, the whole project had grown, becoming his single focus these past few months. And at this point, he didn't know if all the work and study had been more beneficial to William's wife and the children's lives or to his own. All he knew was that if Emma's heart had traversed the same paths as his own, she'd be all right, and he could one day look William in the eyes and tell him that he'd kept the promise he'd made long ago and taken care of Emma and the kids to the best of his ability.

As he watched through the window from his customary spot behind the evergreen, he smiled with satisfaction as her countenance radiated peace, understanding, and gratitude. He personally knew how hard it had been for Emma to face the contents of that box. Coming to know and understand Guillermo's family and his past—next to burying William last Christmas season—had been one of the toughest things he'd ever had to do. But after he'd really looked at them and seen people—not fiends—with tentative and sadder eyes than his own, this process had become much easier, and his own heart had begun to mend. His hopes now strayed to the possibility that not only one family would find healing, but that two would come to find the serenity and hope this season was meant to provide.

As he watched Emma smile and pull out the pen and paper, he knew all would be well this night and that he could continue on with the next phase of his project. Thrusting his hands deep into his red flannel jacket and bowing his head into the snow, he quickly turned and walked down the darkened street to his car knowing that no amount of heat would warm his heart more than what he'd already witnessed tonight.

Emma smiled. She hadn't slept that blissfully in close to a year and, for the first time in about as long, she was genuinely looking forward to the day and what it had to bring. Emma slipped out of her flannel sheets and stepped over to the Venetian blinds, turning them so a bit more sun could brighten the room. Last night's storm had cleared, and nothing but a sea of glistening snow lay for miles and miles upon rooftops, trees, and landscapes.

Had the sky always been this blue, or did it just seem more so today?

It was the first day of Christmas break, and Emma wanted to spend the day living and enjoying life with her children. After calling in to work and taking a personal day, she marched down the hall, whistling, and ordered everyone to report to the kitchen in fifteen minutes.

By the time they all had arrived, Emma had covered her white platter with pancakes and created an all-you-can-eat spread of toppings consisting of honey butter, jams, syrups, cut up fruit, and whipped cream.

"Who gave you a mega caffeine dose?" questioned Jaden as he yawned and scratched his belly.

"And why are you here making pancakes?" asked a baffled Michael, eyeing the new apron Santa had brought him and that Emma had apparently confiscated for the morning. "Aren't you supposed to be getting ready for work or something?"

"Nope. I called in and took a day off so I could spend it here at home with you."

"Who's in trouble?" Jaden looked at each of his siblings, hoping to see a look of guilt on one of their faces that would eliminate him as the culprit.

Emma laughed and flicked a bit of dried batter at him. "No one. I just wanted to spend the day with you making your life as miserable as you've made mine the last dozen years," she chided.

Jaden groaned and then muttered, "Figures . . . I knew I was in trouble for something." He grabbed a full stack of hotcakes and headed to the table so he could drown his sullen attitude in plenty of strawberry syrup.

"No, seriously," Jesse asked before popping the end of a banana rolled in pancake into his mouth.

"Seriously," said Emma as she flipped a cake onto McKenna's plate. "I just wanted to spend the day with you enjoying what we have here together."

Jesse looked at his mother suspiciously. After last night's Santa box experience, he had wondered if she'd be able to remain mentally stable after having faced some of those demons. He now, however, was beginning to wonder if she'd absolutely flipped her lid. She looked okay—one might even say happy—but he knew from having lived with her the past year that this sudden change of spirit could mean one of only three things: she was suffering from some degree of psychosis; he was having a rather pleasant dream; or there was a God and he'd finally given their mother back. Either way, he didn't want to curse the moment, so he jumped in, helping McKenna fix up her pancakes before finishing his own.

Halfway through breakfast (actually it was closer to brunch by this time), the doorbell rang. Racing the kids to the door, Emma swung it open and then realized she stood there in her bathrobe and no makeup. She hadn't known what to expect once she got there—she had just wanted the victory of beating them—but was relieved to find only their Santa box with another letter.

It was only after Emma scanned the front yard looking for any clues that would oust their guest that she noticed the walks had once again been shoveled so not even a footprint was to be had.

Every time it had snowed in the last few weeks, Emma or one of the boys had gone out to clear the walks only to find them already done. Emma had figured it must be one of her neighbors until she realized that the really big snow storms had conveniently coordinated with the arrival of the Santa letters. That was not to say that "Santa" had ordered the storms—they had probably caused a fair amount of grief for him, if he was the one clearing all the snow so as not to leave behind any obvious clues. Emma only hoped that their Christmas visitor had a strong back and knew how grateful she was for the help.

Emma picked up the box and letter and returned to the kitchen. She decided to let the kids go ahead and open the letter so they could read what was in store for them before helping them attack the dishes. Emma knew that Santa wouldn't be foolish enough to tackle that job.

And besides, it was nice for a change to lounge in her bathrobe and slippers, enjoying some quality time with her family.

"I get to do it today." McKenna snatched the letter and tore it open. But after looking at a few of the big words, she quickly handed it over to Michael, who read it aloud.

Jensen Family,

During the holidays, you often hear people wishing others health and good cheer for the coming new year. These are blessings we often wish for each other but seldom really think about until they are taken away.

The Savior, although he was half mortal and half God, never had to deal with physical ailments as many of us do but came to understand the infirmities and limitations of a physical body. Having perfect power over all things physical, he made the blind see, cured leapers, healed the sick, and even raised the dead. He fed those who hungered and gave water to those who thirsted in both a physical and spiritual sense. He still does so today. If we are to learn to become more perfected like him, we need to put aside our physical longings and feast upon his word and thirst for further knowledge.

Health is another one of those words that has many meanings.

There is spiritual health, physical health, mental health, and emotional health. The balance of all of these brings perfect health and good cheer.

How have you been blessed with health, and what does health mean to you? What does good cheer mean? How can you walk in your Savior's shoes, spreading health and good cheer to those around you?

In this box are a few items that you can enjoy while embarking on a trek that will allow you to enjoy health while you receive and spread a bit of Christmas cheer.

I love you, which is why today I want you to celebrate health and good cheer!

Loving always,
Santa

After the last word had been read, McKenna quickly yanked the top off the box and pulled out a set of matching hats, gloves, and scarves for everyone and five punch cards to the Holiday Light and Elf display set up all throughout the downtown area. It was an engaging activity that summoned cheerful participants to follow a trail of clues to Santa's Wonderland. It was something akin to a Christmas version of the ultimate scavenger hunt, only instead of going door to door in a neighborhood, the organizers used the buildings, sidewalks, and sponsoring businesses downtown as the course on which to gather clues that led to a "mystery" warehouse full of craft booths and bargains for last-minute shoppers. Rides, activities, and giant inflatables were also corralled in a secure area for kids' entertainment. The whole course was run through a six-block area and had been started as a way to draw crowds to the downtown area during the holidays. Sponsoring businesses would be "punch points" where "elves" would be stationed giving out clues to the next destination. Business owners loved the traffic, and participants loved an activity that afforded them a bit of Christmas cheer, some pretty good deals, and a place to converge and enjoy their families.

At the end of the event, horse-drawn carriages were even commissioned to take tired participants to the mass transportation stations and the parking lots where their treks had officially begun.

"I guess it was a good day for you to take off, Mom," said Michael as he got up, patted her shoulder, smiled directly at Jaden competitively, and then raced upstairs so he could be the first one to a hot shower.

Emma had never seen so many cheerful people in one place wishing complete strangers a merry Christmas and being so helpful when it came to offering information. There were people of all shapes, sizes, and colors walking along the streets with one goal in mind—to reach their fair city's version of Christmas utopia, Santa's Wonderland. It was amazing how nice people were when they all had the same goal in mind and were willing to help knowing that, for the most part, that assistance would be reciprocated with good tidings during this cheerful time of the year.

Even so, she was pleasantly tired after smiling continuously and being in the thick of life today. She couldn't wait to kick off her boots, curl up in her quilt, and reflect on the past few days while finishing up a few handmade projects.

But as Emma and her small band tromped into the house from the garage, laden with last minute gifts for family and friends, Emma stopped in her tracks and stared at the dishes covering the counter by the sink. She had been right—Santa hadn't been foolish enough to attack that mess. In her excitement to start out on today's adventure, Emma had completely forgotten about cleaning up the kitchen.

Jesse put his bag down and placed his arm around his mother's shoulders. "We were supposed to celebrate health and good cheer, Mom. Mental and emotional health means being able to let the small things go, knowing that your sons will do it in the morning after you go to work."

Emma thankfully nodded at him and smiled as she took McKenna by the hand and headed upstairs to get ready for bed while thinking, "Thank you, God, for such a wonderful family. I could not be more appreciative nor could I have ended this day in a better way."

Emma's thoughts were all awhirl as she drove the familiar route to work. She had a day and a half left to finish out the week before she could join her family for a holiday weekend. And after the way she had rested last night, Emma had no doubts that she could do it with energy to spare. Even though it would be a very sparse Christmas in terms of presents, Emma found herself getting more and more excited about the coming celebration.

As Emma's subconscious went into autopilot, her conscious mind delved a little deeper into some previously unexplored territory. *I wonder if in his day, if all of heaven was this excited knowing that the time of his birth was near or did they even understand the magnitude of such an event as the birth of a Savior for all mankind throughout all generations of time.* Her thoughts having taken that direction proceeded onto a coming day, and she wondered how much of creation would also be excited for his second coming. But before exploring that notion further, Emma was a little caught off guard by the warm, peaceful feeling that drowned her as she quietly understood that it didn't matter. For her and anyone who believed, it would be a glorious day. For the very first time in her life, Emma truly grasped the meaning of the phrase "Thy kingdom come, thy will be done on earth as it is in heaven" in the Lord's Prayer.

So few words and yet so much hope, Emma thought with tears springing to her eyes. A perfect world here on earth like it is there in heaven and one that includes her sweet William to boot. How could anyone keep from shouting with joyful supplication for his kingdom and his glory to come? "And the sooner the better," she added audibly.

By the time she reached work, she was ready to attack the day so she could get back home and see what other insights Santa had in store for her.

Michael called to check in around three o'clock. "We cleaned the house for you, and, yes, that includes scouring the kitchen."

"That's good; otherwise I'd have to make you wait for a really long time to open the next letter and the box."

"You're doing that anyway. Jaden found the box and the next letter around eleven thirty when he took the garbage out. He's been driving us nuts ever since wanting to sneak a peek. Jesse finally had me distract him so he could snatch the box and hide it, but Jaden's been tearing up everything we did in his determination to find it."

"Tell him that for everything out of order when I get home, we wait fifteen minutes while he cleans it back up." Emma pulled the phone away from her ear before Michael's bellows could injure an eardrum. "Well, that was . . . loud."

"Well yeah, I had to get the point across, didn't I? See ya later, Mom, and don't be late!"

Emma smiled and hung up the phone. She didn't need any extra encouragement to get home on time.

"You sure look happy," said Paul. "It's been quite a while since I've seen you smile that much. What gives?"

Paul had been William's closest friend, and he and his wife, Marianne, had become Emma's anchors. It was hard for Emma to hear her own parents lay out her life without William (although it was done out of concern) and look into

Jeanie's grief-stricken eyes, but Paul and Marianne could share Emma's grief without reminding her all the time of what she'd lost. Paul had been there the night William died and was nearly as heartbroken as she herself had been. Since both Paul and William had grown up as only children, they looked to each other as brothers. Had it not been for his wife and their three children, Paul would have been utterly lost after William's death. Emma remembered how, after spending a sleepless night at the hospital, she'd left the room to stretch her legs and go to the public restroom to splash some water on her face. She'd walked back in to a tender scene with William holding Paul's hand telling him how much he loved him and asking him, as his cherished friend, to watch out for Emma and the kids. Paul hadn't had the voice to speak as he combated the colossal lump in his throat but had squeezed William's hand and nodded his head, sealing his promise. As Emma's newly appointed guardian angel, the task Paul had first taken on was to help Emma get her job as the records department manager at the Rocky Mountain Counseling and Family Services Center.

"Oh, it was just a really wonderful day with the kids yesterday. I took the day off, and I thoroughly enjoyed the time with them for the first time in a really long time. I didn't know if I'd ever be able to enjoy Christmastime again after last year, but yesterday proved me wrong."

Paul patted her shoulder and smiled. "I'm glad, Emma. I know William is probably reveling in seeing you smile again."

Paul and Marianne had been very concerned about Emma and had talked hours on end about what to do for her. Paul had played the moment he'd promised William he'd look out for Emma and the kids over and over in his mind and had felt like a total failure the past few months as he watched the life drain out of her eyes day by day. When Marianne had finally come to him just as worried, he decided that something had to be done. They'd gone to visit Emma at the onset of autumn, knowing how hard this time of year would be for her. As they visited with her, Paul had gained a new respect for Emma as she'd managed to survive under all the stress and heartache. He himself had barely kept it together as he ran a hand across the reference books he and William had spent hours studying together. Every now and then, as he and Marianne visited with Emma and the kids, Paul would go into William's home office just so he could feel close to his old buddy.

But over the course of the last few weeks, Paul had seen

a definite change in Emma and knew that all of his hard work and prayers had been worth it.

Emma stepped through the back door and called, "I'm home! Let the festivities begin!"

There was a thundering on the steps as her three rather large boys and petite little girl pounded down the stairs, heading for the front room, where the box awaited.

"Hey, you goons. I meant food. I'm hungry. Who's going to help me with dinner?"

"It's done. I did it myself," grinned Jaden.

Emma scowled and cocked an eyebrow at Jaden, who was known for melting pans as he boiled them dry while making hard boiled eggs. Emma knew that if he hadn't actually attempted to cook tonight's meal, the menu would probably be something along the lines of peanut butter and jelly sandwiches again.

She quickly headed for the kitchen but broke into fit of laughter when she looked at a box of Cheerios placed neatly in the center of the table between a bunch of bananas and a gallon of milk. He'd even gone to the trouble of setting out placemats along with the bowls and spoons.

"Well, so it is. Let's eat then," Emma said and pulled out her chair.

Needless to say, dinner and cleanup didn't take long at all. Jaden slurped his cereal down in record time, grabbed everyone else's bowls, and tossed them into the dishwasher.

"I told you he went nuts after Jesse hid the letter and box," Michael leaned over and whispered to his mother. She just smiled as she grabbed a rag to wipe off the table before heading in by the tree.

"Jaden, since you've been so helpful, why don't you do us the honor?" Emma motioned to the letter and box Jesse was bringing into the room. Jaden leaped over the coffee table, nearly toppling a candlestick as Emma cringed but managed to hold her tongue.

"You betcha! It's been just about killing me today. I think for the first time in my life even I appreciated that school was useful for something," Jaden admitted as he took the box and letter from Jesse.

Emma steadied her candlestick. "And just what have you come to decide school is useful for?"

"Keeping my mind off these flippin' letters and

boxes!" he said as he ripped open the next Santa letter.

Jensen Family,

You come from a long line of good people. They represent your heritage. Your physical characteristics, your mannerisms, your religion and customs—they are all handed down to you from the past.

Christ had a wonderful heritage too. To those who'd been righteous and whom the Lord especially loved, he promised that the Savior would be born through their bloodlines—they would become the Savior's heritage. Joseph of Egypt and King David both took great pride in knowing the importance their heritage, or bloodlines, would be to the world.

Have you honored your heritage as your ancestors have honored you? Think of what you have learned from those who have gone before you. What are the lessons they have taught, and what can you take from them?

Jaden, you recently had to do a report on your family's heritage and how it was important to the state you live in. What did you learn?

Jesse, you are one of the few grandchildren who can remember so many wonderful things about and interactions with your great-grandparents. What do you most remember?

Michael and McKenna, what can you remember about your grandparents, and what lessons from their lives do you want to take into your own?

There are a few items in this box that will help you celebrate your heritage by remembering how important these people are to you and, as you do so, they in turn will be proud as you demonstrate and discuss how you have taken the lessons they've taught and applied them to your own lives.

I love you, which is why tonight I want you to celebrate a good heritage and all the wonderful things that have been passed down to you.

Loving always,
Santa

The letter had barely touched the ground before Jaden slipped the top off the box and pulled out a DVD case with another envelope taped to the top and addressed to "The Jensens." They also found packets of spiced apple cider, some popcorn, and chocolate covered pretzels. Jaden opened the next envelope.

Jensens,

I have arranged for you to spend a night at your grandparents' so they can share stories and pictures with you about your ancestors. You are then cordially invited to watch this special DVD that has been made for you to help you remember that even though people come and go, families are like a chain—each member being a link that remains connected forever.

Hurry, your grandparents are waiting!

Santa

As the kids scurried to gather coats, Emma grabbed her purse and keys, anxious to get to her in-laws' home. She had one thought on her mind—if "Santa" had arranged with them to participate in this night, maybe they'd finally have their first clue as to who had given them such a wonderful and memorable Christmas. The excitement of figuring out the mystery made her step on the gas pedal a little harder.

Jeanie had Walter running all over the place getting ready for the night. Ever since she'd found out that they were to be a part of this journey Emma and the kids were going through, she hadn't rested—or allowed Walter to either—wanting to make sure everything was perfect. "Only one more thing to do," Walter grumbled as he checked another item off the list Jeanie had given him. He grabbed the sack out of the garbage compactor and headed out the back door.

"Hey, Walter, aren't you usually gone by now?" his neighbor Hy questioned as he poked his head over the fence.

"Not tonight, my friend. Emma and the kids are coming over here for an activity," he chuckled.

"So I s'pose you won't be needin' those items tonight," guessed Hy.

"Nope, not unless Jeanie drives me nuts with her projects and I need an excuse to run out the door."

"Well, you know the entry code to the garage. They're there if you need 'em," Hy called over his shoulder. "The wife and I are headin' out to finish up some shopping, but make yourself at home if you need to." He laughed before turning around and adding, "And, uh, Walter, enjoy the night with your family. It's about you and Jeanie as much as it is about Emma and the kids, you know . . ."

"Yeah, I know, and we're getting there. I can see Jeanie is excited about the night, which does my old ticker good. It's been good having a semblance of normalcy again after the last year."

"Well, if anyone deserves it, Walter, it's your family. I know how hard you've worked for it."

"Thanks, Hy. Have a good time shopping tonight." Walter waved as he headed back inside.

Jeanie was at the door ready to greet her son's family. After his death, it had been rather awkward as the two women who'd loved him most grieved, each afraid of saying anything that would reopen wounds that were healing far too slowly as it was. But tonight was a step into the future, and Jeanie hadn't realized how much she'd missed the laughter and presence of his family since William's tragic accident. She thought back on the letter she and Walter had read and became increasingly excited. This night would be her chance to remember with gratitude the lives they'd shared and the relationships that entwined them.

"Well hello, my little darlings," Jeanie called and scurried out to wrap her arms around her grandchildren and Emma. After Emma had helped McKenna take off her boots and hang up her coat, she went into the kitchen, where Jeanie was emptying the last bag of popcorn into a huge bowl.

Emma eased into the conversation. "Jeanie, how have

you dealt with the last year? I mean, at times, as I'm sure you know, I've barely been able to cope . . ."

Jeanie had known questions would come and had prepared for them. "It's been very hard, but I've found the best way to deal with it has been one step and one day at a time while trying to find the small joys in life."

"I know what you mean. I didn't think I'd ever be able to survive this year, let alone the dreaded one-year anniversary, but something magical and wonderful has happened that's managed to ease my burdens. I've even been able to find gratitude and the will to live again."

"Could it have anything to do with tonight?" Jeanie smiled and handed her daughter-in-law the bowl.

Emma perked up. "Yes, actually. By the way, how did you find out about tonight? Did you talk to anyone?"

"Oh, no. It was quite a curious thing really," Jeanie smiled. "I was coming home from my watercolor class when I found this letter on the front porch instructing us on what we needed to do to help complete a special project."

"Was it signed?"

"Yes, with the initials *SC* and then an explanation: 'someone who cares.' "

"Oh, I see." Emma didn't know if she was feeling twinges

of disappointment or relief for being no closer to solving the mystery of their Christmas guest.

"Let's go on downstairs, Em. Papa's got the old movie projector and slide viewer set up for the show of your life!"

"Was that a really bad pun?" Emma smiled.

"Not on purpose, but it was kind of clever, wasn't it?" Jeanie hooked her arm through Emma's and escorted her downstairs.

Emma had watched the DVD of her and William's life together over and over again until it continued playing throughout the night in her dreams. All of her family living on the East Coast had wanted to be of assistance in the days before William's funeral, and so they had taken upon themselves the project of putting together a tribute to play during his viewing.

Emma hadn't been able to watch it then or ever since because she was afraid that if she did, his favorite songs that framed those happy images would beckon her back to a life she couldn't ever have again. On the night of his viewing, watching even a few seconds of it had made her want to follow William's trail. But last night, as she watched it with his parents and her children, Emma found herself being thankful for having had such a wonderful life with such a wonderful man. For the too-brief years they'd had together, they'd had some amazing adventures and had lived a love story most could only dream of. She couldn't wait to pick up where they'd left off as they continued their courtship into eternity. Life, after all, was a pretty short moment in time compared to eternity, and Emma was beginning to think that she could do anything for a just moment—that is, until they could be reunited again.

Shaking off the sleepiness while hanging onto the warm feelings, Emma whispered, "Good morning to you too, William. Be sure to watch out for our children today while I'm not home. Jaden's been rather rambunctious lately, and I don't know if Jesse's or Michael's patience can survive much more." She listened to the reassuring silence for a bit longer, also noting that she was glad she'd hung in there and survived the last year, before getting up and scrambling off to the shower.

"Did you have to hide the box and letter again?" asked Emma when Jesse called.

"He doesn't even know it came. He slept in, so I took advantage of that fact and hid it before he could even find out it'd been delivered. I figured I'd give 'Santa' a bit of help since Jaden bragged that today was the day Santa would be unmasked."

"He did, did he? What made him so sure?"

"When he finally did get up, he rigged the camcorder from the garage window so he could record any movement."

"Did he get anything?"

"Nope, this character is pretty dang smart! It's a good thing though that the letter and items were delivered early this morning. He always seems to be one step ahead of us. It kinda makes you wonder . . ." Jesse teased his mother.

"That it does," Emma firmly countered, thinking how relieved she'd been last night when Jeanie's answers had allowed the Christmas enchantment to remain intact for Emma. "But sometimes mysteries are best when they remain unsolved. It allows the magic to live on forever."

By the time Emma had reached the end of her work day, she'd had nine calls from Jaden, who'd spent his entire day watching through his camcorder lens. "I know he won't disappoint us. I-I think he's doing this on purpose just to drive me batty."

"Jaden, how do you know it's a he? Couldn't it be a she?"

"Heck no! Then the letters would be signed Mrs. C."

"Oh, I see, as a twelve-year-old, you have all the answers, don't you?"

"Just hurry home. They're *always* here by the time you get home," emphasized Jaden before hanging up.

Emma smiled. Jaden had been the one she most worried about when William died because of his tendency to bottle things up. Only William had been able to get Jaden to open up and sort through his emotions, and when William couldn't, Jaden would clam up until he exploded. She'd feared how Jaden would handle things and wondered if Christmas would forever be ruined for him. Emma could only send silent prayers of thanks for whoever had planned this series of Christmas events and surprises, rescuing her emotionally immature twelve-year-old. "Santa" had not only pulled her out of a living grave but had opened the hearts of all of her children, making the season a time to reflect and remember just exactly what the real gifts of Christmas were rather than having it be a time to mourn.

Knowing how anxious they'd be to get on with their night, Emma promised to grab a couple of pizzas if Jesse would make a salad. Michael had offered to set the table and clean up while Jaden stayed glued to the viewfinder of his camera.

Emma hadn't yet pressed the garage opener's button before Jaden had the door open and was storming her car.

"He hasn't come yet. We can't be done! There's supposed to be three more days!"

Emma took pity on Jaden, although she momentarily feared for Jesse's well-being. "It came early this morning. Jesse hid it again rather than put up with your constant needling and attempts to sneak a couple of peeks."

Emma needn't have feared; Jaden's relieved sigh said it all. "Whew, I thought he'd forgotten about us." He kissed his mother on the cheek, grabbed the pizza boxes, and headed in with a piece already halfway gone.

With the boxes empty and the minor mess cleaned up, the family headed into the living room, where Jesse had finally placed the Santa items. Tonight Emma decided to take a turn reading the letter:

Jensen Family,

Those who are the happiest people upon the earth are those who seek richness in souls rather than the wealth of the world. To give of oneself is the most noble of gifts a person can give.

Service to God and your fellowmen is the key to happiness and eternal life. Even Christ taught, "He that findeth his life shalt lose it, and he that loseth his life for my sake shall find it." He meant that the person who finds happiness and peace in life has found it because he has lost so much of himself through service and charity. That same person will find eternal life because he followed the Savior's example by giving of himself and serving his fellowmen.

If people would just learn to forget themselves and serve one another, this world would be healed one heart at a time. For people who serve one another learn to love one another, and in doing so, both the giver and the receiver grow closer to God with more of a chance to return home and live with him again one day.

Without service and love, there is nothing left but selfishness and hate.

Your Savior's whole life was about service—there is no better model to follow when serving others. This King of Kings washed the feet of others, fed multitudes, and spent endless hours teaching. And then when the appointed time had come, he also willingly gave his worldly dignity, blood, and life for others. Is there any better example of true service than this man we call Christ?

How do you feel when you have unselfishly given of yourself? Do you go to bed with a smile on your face and warmth in your heart? How do you think the receiver of such service feels?

One of the most beautiful parts of the body is the hands, for it is these that a mother uses to caress her children, a father to tickle his youngsters, the young to care for the elderly, and the elderly to show young ones the way. Hands are an extension of the heart when performing service. And in our Savior's case—where imprints mar the hollow of his perfect hand—a reminder of his sacrifice for us.

In this box are six pairs of utility gloves to protect your hands. I want you to put them in a visible place, reminding you to make service a priority in the coming months as you spread Christmas's holiday cheer throughout the year. In a year, I also want you to be able to say that you've worn the gloves out while having grown stronger by helping those along the way.

I love you, which is why tonight I want you to ponder service—that which has been done for you and that which you can do for others. Find yourselves by losing yourselves in service.

Loving always,
Santa

Michael, who had taken possession of the box, pulled out a pair of gloves for each family member and handed them around. Silence filled the room until McKenna ever so timidly stole the moment. "Mama, do you know Santa's number?"

"Why do you need his number, sweetie?"

"So I can call him."

Emma smiled. "Well, I know that, but why do you need to call him?"

"Because there is a boy at my school in Mrs. Bailey's class named Trevor Bryant who died and went to heaven like Daddy."

Everyone looked at McKenna with puzzled expressions. Emma quickly got down on her knees in front of her little girl so she could see eye to eye as she asked, "Kenna, what does that have to do with needing to call Santa?"

"Well, I figure if their hearts hurt as much as ours did, then I want to do something to help them feel better like Santa did for us. I know Santa was going to find a way to bring Daddy home for the holidays, but I want him to bring their little boy instead. They need to know that Jesus is taking care of him now."

Emma was speechless. She'd known how much McKenna believed in miracles—especially those involving the magic of Christmas—but in McKenna's mind, it was an absolute that William would be returning home for the holidays. Visualizing the disappointment in her little girl's eyes had broken Emma's spirit before their own Christmas miracle had begun. It had renewed not only Emma's faith by giving her hope, but by also giving her children their mother back. All of Emma's swirling thoughts righted themselves as she began to envision another scene—a clear picture in her mind of what needed to be done. Just as someone had given them the gift of hope, Emma and the kids would give this family the same.

"Honey, let's not bother Santa. He's so busy with it being so close to Christmas, so let's do something special like he's done for us and put his name on the card."

"You mean we'll be like his elves?"

"No, I mean we *will* be his elves!" Emma told the boys to run to the grocery store and grab some blue construction paper, about fifty tea light candles, a white and a baby-blue helium balloon, and a bag of Hershey's kisses. Emma grabbed McKenna by the hand.

"Where are we going?"

"To do something very special, my little one."

When the boys returned home, Emma set aside the special project she and McKenna had been working on and went down to direct the rest of the efforts. She had all four of them trace and cut out their handprints and then help her carry everything to the car. Emma grabbed the bag she had set by the back door containing what she and McKenna had worked on and a jar full of kisses with a baby-blue bow tied around the neck of the jar.

When they reached the Bryants' house, Emma parked her car up the street so they could tiptoe to the front yard unnoticed. Michael set down the handprints in a big heart shape while Jaden placed a candle on the palm of each one. Emma tied the balloons to the paw of a bear she'd been given when William had died. It had the most angelic face, a blue baseball cap, and a set of gossamer wings. McKenna then handed her mother the verse Emma had written and that McKenna had copied in her childish scrawl. Emma rolled it up into a scroll and placed it under the little bear's arm. With their task completed, Emma handed her daughter the bear. McKenna kissed his furry nose and whispered, "Help them to be happy and not miss

Trevor so much," before placing him in a basket that was lined with a soft baby-blue blanket. As Emma, McKenna, and Michael headed for the car, Jesse finished lighting each of the candles as Jaden rang the doorbell, and then they both disappeared into the night. Once everyone had been accounted for, Emma put the car into neutral and coasted down the back side of the hill, hoping that the Bryant family, too, would find a little bit of comfort in some Christmas magic.

Deborah Bryant felt hollow. Her worst fear had been realized when the police showed up at her door, telling her about the accident. Trevor had been on his way to a friend's house when, in his excitement, he'd darted out in front of a car. The driver had not even had time to brake.

Every day she fought with feelings of failure. Why hadn't she driven him? Why hadn't she taught him traffic rules and safety better? The loss was so acute, it was sometimes hard to breathe. If only she could know that her baby was okay and had somehow forgiven her for failing to protect him and keep him safe.

As tears poured down her cheeks, she faintly heard

the doorbell ring. A few minutes later, her husband came into the room and said, "Honey, I think you'd better come see this." Deborah picked up her baby girl, Abbie, and grabbed three-year-old Ally's hand and walked to the front door. She handed the baby off to her husband and walked among the small handprints. As she looked back at her trail, she realized it was in the shape of a heart. She moved to the bear in the middle and, as she picked him up, a scroll tied with a blue bow fell out. She undid the bow and read,

> *My hands hold little lights*
> *So you can easily see*
> *That I'm not all alone here;*
> *Jesus is walking with me.*
> *But he lets me come say hello*
> *Every now and again*
> *So I can give you kisses*
> *Letting you know my love I send.*
>
> *I love you forever and ever,*
> *Trevor*

Deborah fell to her knees in the snow, hugging the bear tightly to her chest. She looked upward toward heaven and, with a barely audible voice due to the large lump swelling in her throat, mouthed the words "thank you" for letting her know that her little boy was being well taken care of and was not as far off as she had once imagined.

That night everyone came in the back door and headed straight to the living room to stare at their stack of Santa letters under the tree illuminated by the white twinkling lights. No one said a word. Each kissed Emma on the cheek, said good night, and headed up the stairs. No one had needed to say a word. The magic of the night spoke volumes and left them all with serenity, a sense of thankfulness, and feelings of love, wonder, and appreciation for having been part of something so special.

Emma pulled out her scalloped-edged quilt, thinking about all the gifts they'd received this year. She was temporarily saddened by the thought that it was almost over until she realized that, in actuality, it had just begun. They would not be receiving Santa letters and seeing what the box was filled with every night, but they had the lessons they'd learned and the growth they'd obtained as a family. She felt closer than ever to William and realized that with a little work, they could keep this spirit, this knowledge, and these wonderful feelings alive well beyond Christmas day. After all, if she were to follow the Savior's example by giving what she could, it needn't necessarily be on only one day a year. Through the many small and simple opportunities to serve every day of the year, Emma knew her family could keep this spirit alive.

Emma was getting tired and still had a few things to complete. She pulled her quilt tight about her and headed up the stairs. Tomorrow, after all, was Christmas Eve.

❄ ❄ ❄

"It's here! It's here!" McKenna yelled at the top of her lungs, making sure no one could sleep through her announcement.

Michael drowsily clamored out into the hallway. "What's here?"

"The next Santa letter."

"Already? Wow, this guy sure travels fast. Our feet are barely warmed from last night." Michael went to rouse Jaden, who apparently had found a way to sleep through

McKenna's commotion. Jesse stretched and yawned as he stumbled to the bathroom. Jaden and Emma were the next ones up.

"What in the world are you bellowing about?" Emma asked groggily.

"The next Santa letter—it's here!"

"Already? Wow, that . . ."

"I know, I know; he travels fast. Michael already said that."

Emma snapped her jaw shut and looked down the hall at Michael as he came out of his and Jaden's room and shrugged his shoulders.

"Well, let's go read it so we know what today holds," Emma reasoned.

This time they all gathered on top of Emma's bed, burying their cold feet in her covers. "Kenna, with a little help, would you read this one for us?"

McKenna smiled and opened the letter. She read in a rather loud and deliberate tone.

Jensen Family,

What would this world be without family? Where would you be without family? And what truly is a family?

A family is more than just a group of people living in the same household. It is more than people who share a common ancestor or relative. It is much more than a string of people on a pedigree chart.

These are people who have been tied at the heart throughout generations of time and space. Whether you wish it to be so or not, their blood, genes, and heritage have been passed on to you, and, for better or worse, you take what they have to offer and can add goodness to it so that future generations can continue adding upon it also.

The Savior referred to each and every one of us as his brother or sister, knowing that we share the same parentage—a perfect Father in Heaven. What better family ties could you have than that? You are literally the offspring of God! Despite what you face here on earth, how could you deny your potential when you come from such royal lineage and such perfect parentage?

But you have been especially blessed because, not only do you have a regal heritage, but you also have been blessed with a good family here upon the earth.

A few nights ago, you learned about your heritage and those who've paved the way before, but tonight you will celebrate your family both immediate and extended as you gather around a Christmas tree to laugh, ponder, and remember your family—

especially a brother whose birth it is we commemorate this and every Christmas season.

I love you, which is why tonight I want you to take this food and go enjoy the blessings of family.

Loving always,
Santa

Inside the box was all the fixings for a vegetable tray, a gelatin salad, and spiced punch.

Emma barely had time to process the instructions before the phone rang. "Hey, Em," greeted Walter. "According to this letter I got in my hand, I s'pose we're coming over there. It was attached to a ham, a bag of rolls, and a bunch of other trappin's, so I guess that means I'll hafta fight those boys of yours off for a scrap or two to make a sandwich." Emma laughed as she heard Jeanie in the background scolding him for being so rude. "What're you talking about? Rude? Mother, you know as well as I that they're growing boys and that means endless pits . . ."

"Good thing it's a huge ham then. A little bit of competition never stopped you from getting your fair share,"

Jeanie chidingly scoffed from the background.

Walter grumbled and returned to the phone. "So what time are we going to start this shindig?"

"How about five o'clock? I have a few errands I still need to wrap up today."

"Us too. Apparently we got two more things to pick up . . ."

"We'll see you at five then—and drive carefully. William used to drive like a madman when he was in a good mood, and I know where he got that from!"

"Oh women! Ya'll worry too much," he chuckled. "See you later, dear."

"Bye, Walter." Emma hung up the phone and, as she did, couldn't help but think for a moment about what she and William would've been like in their twilight years. But quickly realizing there was no time to waste, she scampered off to the kitchen, wolfed down what was left of the banana-walnut muffins Michael had made, and headed upstairs to get ready for the day.

As Emma bustled around trying to get her errands done, she couldn't help but think about the events of the past year. It had certainly been a year of extremes, a year she never would have asked for, but as she looked back, she could now see all the many tender moments that had allowed her to find strength and hope. There was only one thing she wished she could change. "That would be the ability to be with you, my love," she smiled sadly as she headed out to complete her one last errand.

After entering the cemetery, Emma drove to the third tree on the right-hand side of the fork that veered to the left. She didn't have to count the trees anymore; it was instinctual by now, she realized as she put her car into park. Grabbing the envelope, she walked to the fourth row and brushed what was left of the snow off his marker.

"Well, love, it's been a year. I just needed a few minutes alone with you today to let you know how much I love you—forever and always—and how much I miss you. I don't have much time, but I wanted to bring you this." Emma opened the envelope, making sure that the heart-shaped piece Emma had cut out from their old quilt was still tucked neatly inside the love letter to her husband. "I explained everything in here." She held up the envelope before placing it in the metal urn she'd lifted out of the ground, turned over, and secured tightly at the head of his stone. "But somehow I think you already know and approve," she said, smiling. Emma then blew a kiss to heaven before returning to the warmth of her car.

At a quarter to five the doorbell rang. Emma looked at the clock and grinned. For years, Walter had always been fifteen minutes early because Jeanie, when they had first married, had turned all of their clocks ahead so her perpetually late husband would find his way home and to events on time. Even though his sense of time had vastly improved over the years and Jeanie's secret had long been ousted, Walter still ran his life according to MST—Mother's Standard Time, which was always fifteen minutes early.

When Emma opened the door, she had quite a surprise waiting for her. There on the doorstep stood her own parents, who had traveled all the way from North Carolina. Emma was thrilled to see them, having been able to finally hear the love and concern in their voices over the course of the last few weeks rather than what she'd taken to be as a barrage of painful criticisms. As she'd looked at her own children and their lives, realizing what she wanted for them and what she would sacrifice for them, she couldn't help but be warmed and renewed by the constant love her parents had shown her the last year—even if she hadn't initially taken it that way.

"I told you we had two more things to pick up," Walter chuckled and brushed past the group to head on down the hall.

"What are you doing here?" Emma beamed and hugged each of them before taking their coats.

"Well, about a month ago, we got this mysterious—"

"Letter? Yeah, we know a lot about those around here," laughed Emma. "Either way, I'm glad you're here."

While Emma and the kids caught up with her parents, Walter quietly stole back into the family room, where Emma had placed the few presents she'd managed to acquire under the family tree. Walter looked at each ornament that had been hung, but he stopped at the one McKenna had made last year with painted and glittered popsicle sticks framing a copy of the family picture they'd had taken the fall before. Walter missed his son more than he could ever explain, but what had kept him going was the promise he'd made the day William was born to keep a vigilant and watchful eye over his son. As William had grown and eventually had a family of his own, Walter renewed his promise, expanding the duties of his ever watchful eye to now include Emma and the kids. Now they were his family too, and he loved them every bit as much as he had loved his own son. "No doubt at all," Walter murmured under his breath as he looked at the children in the photo who carried so many traits of their father and other members of their family.

He slipped his hand inside the front pocket of his jacket and pulled out a letter that was attached to a thin oblong box. Both were secured with a golden bow. Walter fluffed the bow so it didn't look quite so crushed and bent down to hide it under the other packages, where it would be well out of sight for the time being.

"What are you doing, you old codger?" Jeanie quizzed him. "Are you doin' what I think you're doin'?"

"Oh, humph. Well, okay, you caught me." He winked and then continued, "I was seeing what the kids were gettin' for Christmas and if I needed to sneak out and get something more."

"Right. Did you hide it well enough that they won't see it until tomorrow?"

Walter smiled and winked over his shoulder. He'd never been able to fool his Jeanie. "I better have or all the work will have lost some of its magical luster."

Jeanie moved over to help her husband up off his knees so she could hug him. "You'll never change, will you? There'll always be a little bit of a Santa in you, and that's one of the reasons I love you so much."

It had been a wonderful night full of laughter, stories, food, and fun. Emma had looked around at all the faces surrounding her and thanked her lucky stars that she'd found enough favor in God's eyes to have been blessed with this blissfully kooky group of good-hearted people. As she watched her children laugh and enjoy their grandparents, Emma had truly felt as if William really wasn't that far off. Jesse's voice, having finally deepened, was so much like his father's, and Michael's work ethic, morning personality, and love of the kitchen sometimes transported her back to Saturday mornings when she'd wake up to the smell of pancakes and sausage or bacon. And Jaden had that childlike mischievousness that was so typical of his father, while McKenna had her daddy's caring heart and absolute faith.

Figuring that their old bones needed a bit more rest than the grandkids were likely to give, Emma's parents had accepted Walter's invitation to sleep at their house. "I'll have Mother whip up a batch of her French toast though," promised Walter, "and your mom has carte blanche to whatever she needs to pop out a couple dozen of her famous cinnamon rolls. We'll be here to take over when you're about ready to go back to bed."

"It's a deal then." Emma hugged each of her parents as they slipped out the door into another storm. Walter grabbed ahold of Jeanie's elbow and looked toward the billowing skies. "I'm glad you don't need to sneak over to Hy's to borrow his ratty old red coat and hat," Jeanie whispered. "Tonight we'll celebrate a job well done by a warm fire," she said as she put her arm around his waist and helped him lead the group to their car.

After Emma had made sure all of the kids were asleep, she pulled out one last item from under her bed. She'd wanted to make something for the kids that would show them how much she and William loved them. The children were their touchstone, giving them the strength they needed to face the world. The idea had come to her the night she'd learned about Guillermo Menendez and his family. That was the night she'd opened her heart to the possibilities of moving on as she counted her blessings—one of those being the knowledge that this life was not all there was but merely a stepping stone placed upon a path that takes us through a wonderful journey throughout eternity.

She'd stayed up the last few nights to finish this project, and with a few more hours, it would be complete, wrapped, and under the tree waiting for her children on Christmas morning.

As was expected, McKenna was up early—so early it couldn't even be considered morning yet.

"Mama, get up! We get to see what Santa brought!"

Emma rolled over and stretched as she looked at the clock. After finishing her project, wrapping the remaining presents, and setting out McKenna's gift from Santa, she'd finally made it to bed forty-five minutes ago.

"Are the boys up yet?"

"No, they won't get up until you are up!"

"Well, let's go get them up then." Emma kicked off her covers, grasped McKenna's hand, and raced down the hall.

McKenna had been thrilled with the bike Santa brought and had fortunately not noticed that it was the neighbor girl's hand-me-down decked out with a new seat, bell, water bottle holder, basket, and a few sparkly stickers. To McKenna it was perfect!

Considering their circumstances, the boys were fine with the necessary replacement items like socks, underwear, T-shirts, and a pair of jeans. Their eyes couldn't help but wander, though, to the last package under the tree—the one Emma had put there less than a couple of hours ago.

"Mom, who is that one for?" asked Michael, nudging his head in the general direction of the last unwrapped and rather large gift.

"It's for all of us," said Emma as she motioned for Jesse to retrieve it from under the tree. Each of the children then tore at a corner, revealing what Emma had worked so painstakingly to accomplish over the last week. In a huge frame made of antique wood was their family portrait with appliquéd letters underneath it that spelled out "Our Family Will Be Together Forever." Below that was another saying, in much smaller stitching, that read, "Families are like old quilts. Even though they may unravel at times, they can always be stitched back together with love and patience."

The picture and the sayings were highlighted against a backdrop of a beautiful, although well-worn, patchwork quilt. It was a familiar pattern—one they'd seen many times before.

"Mom, isn't that your and dad's special quilt?" quizzed Jesse.

"Yes, it is."

"But why would you cut it up to do something like this?"

"Because, Jesse, it's not the quilt that meant so much to me, it's what it represented—all of our good times, warmth when we needed it, heritage since Grandma made it out of old clothes belonging to the people we've loved, family traditions since it went on every trip and picnic with us.

"We've had such a magical Christmas. We've had the opportunity to remember all these wonderful things made possible by a loving God who also sent us the ultimate offering in the form of his Son. I wanted to capture it and put it in a place where we could all remember the true gifts of Christmas and why it is we celebrate this day. I want us all to remember that the best gift of Christmas is life—our life together, life beyond the grave, and life everlasting—and I want us to celebrate it not just during the holidays, but each and every day."

"I know where it should go," Michael said as he grabbed

the frame and asked Jesse and Jaden to follow him. Jesse grabbed a hammer and nails and told Jaden to grab a step-stool.

Michael and Jesse then moved the small table in the front entryway and positioned the picture above their family mission statement so Jaden could mark where the nail should go.

After Jesse had hung it on the wall, they all stood back and admired Emma's handiwork. "Now as we leave or come home, we'll remember what's important, what we're grateful for, and what we should be celebrating every day," said Michael, smiling.

Emma hugged her children, sighed, and then verbalized just one more Christmas wish: "I just wish we could see your dad and know for sure that he was here celebrating Christmas with us. Oh well, I guess I'll just have to go on faith that he's here in spirit."

McKenna tugged on her bathrobe. "The day's not over yet, Mama."

Emma framed her daughter's face with her hand, amazed at the perfect faith McKenna always seemed to display. "You're right, sweetheart. If we listen very closely, we might hear Daddy whispering 'Merry Christmas' from heaven."

Emma smiled down at her daughter before heading to the kitchen to start on breakfast. "Will you all please pick up the wrapping paper and tidy up the family room?"

As Emma pulled out all she would need to make crepes (another Jensen family holiday tradition) from the cupboards, the boys picked up all the wrapping paper, bows, and boxes. McKenna, being the smallest, climbed between the couch and the tree, where she spotted a golden bow. She reached back as far as she could, grabbed the end with her small fingers, and pulled it toward her.

"It's here! Our last Santa letter! It's here!" squealed McKenna in childish excitement as she bounded around the room, holding the letter and box out for everyone to see.

Emma hurried from the kitchen. "Where was it, Kenna?"

"Way, way back under the tree. I barely saw it."

Emma thought about the night before as she'd arranged the packages, hoping to make them look more plentiful than her budget had allowed. She hadn't seen this package there, however. She supposed that she could've missed it as she pulled and arranged things, possibly scooting it even farther into the corner where McKenna had found it. Even more bothersome, though, was how it'd gotten under the tree in the first place. Emma mentally calculated how many people—family, friends, and even strangers—had been in this room. She tried to deduce who the sly guest had been. In the recesses of her heart, though, she didn't really want to know, and so after another few moments of thought, she reminded herself that whoever had given them such a magical season had not disappointed them yet, nor was their Christmas benefactor likely to. It didn't matter how it'd gotten under the tree. What mattered was that it had given Emma and her family one more cherished day of yuletide magic.

"Kenna, you found it, so why don't you open it?" advised Emma.

McKenna opened the letter, but after scanning a few words that could be perceived as intimidating to a first grader, she quickly handed it over to her mother.

Jensen Family,

You have experienced eleven days of Christmas that have reminded you of the gifts of warmth; music; traditions; laughter; friendship; support; justice, mercy, and forgiveness; health and good cheer; heritage; service; and family. But this last gift I chose to hold until Christmas morning since it is the most significant of all the gifts you have—a parent's love.

It is not only a knowledge of your earthly parents' love but that also of your heavenly parents: "For God so loved the world that he gave his only Begotten Son."

Your parents have nourished you, comforted you, taught you, chided you, and, when the time comes, they will let you go to make your own way in the world so that you too may progress and grow, creating your own little pieces of heaven here on earth. They will also be there to welcome you back home with open arms when the world seems a bit too overwhelming and you simply need a rest.

Your Father in Heaven is the same. He nourished you, comforted you, taught you, and even chided you before he knew the day would come when he'd have to let you go so you could learn and grow and one day become like him. He will also be there to welcome you home with open arms when this world has made you weary and you have earned your rest.

The greatest work and glory any loving parent strives for is the perfection of their children. You are your parents'—both earthly and heavenly—work and glory, and both want nothing more than for your success.

Success is why a plan was presented and ratified, a plan to allow us to learn through agency and live in this world while still maintaining—for those of us who choose to do so—our celestial ties. A Savior balanced those scales for us while his parents—both here on this earth and in heaven—ached excruciatingly at the pain their Son had to endure for the greater good so that all of God's children could one day return home and abide with him once again.

I love you, which is why I have given you these twelve days to enjoy. But your Heavenly Father loves you more, and that is why he gave you a Savior. It is his birth and a parent's love we commemorate this time each year.

Jensens, as the days turn into a new year, remember the true gifts of Christmas and take what you have learned into each new day. Remember Christmas and put more Christ into your everyday lives.

Loving always,
Santa

The room was silent until McKenna, after looking around at everyone, took it upon herself to open the oblong box. There were five more letters, the first of which had Emma's name printed in a golden script. Those underneath had the same golden script but spelled out each of the children's names. Emma looked around at each one of her children and then carefully handed each one their special letter.

Emma, trying to understand the meaning of this last gift, watched as each of her children opened their letters and read them silently. As tears welled up in each of their eyes, and smiles intermingled with joy and a bit of longing spread across their faces, Emma couldn't resist and broke the seal on hers.

She looked at the familiar handwriting and covered her mouth with a trembling hand. She scanned down to the signature, wanting to make sure it was not a cruel hoax, but . . . there it was: "Eternally yours with all the love a man can possess, William."

As time stood still and her background faded, she could clearly hear her beloved's gentle voice as she read.

My dearest Emmie,

Words will never be adequate enough to let you know of my love and appreciation for you. From the first day I met you, I felt as if I'd finally come home. You are the one who has always been my anchor, my support, my strength, and my loving touchstone to all that is real, important, and eternal. I cannot imagine life, or death for that matter, without you.

As we celebrate this Christmas together, the holiday that celebrates the birth of our Savior who made being with you and the kids forever a possibility, I want you to know that no matter how many miles separate us, no matter how many moments are stolen away from us by worldly time bandits robbing us of laughter and placing challenges before us to sidetrack our dreams, I will always be here with you, loving you, watching over you, and protecting you.

You are the one who completes me and makes me a whole man. And for that, neither heaven nor earth's boundaries can, or ever will, come between us.

Eternally yours with all the love a man can possess,
William

Emma held the tear soaked letter to her chest and in a barely audible voice said, "I love you too, William." Emma turned to look at the small hand that had been gently placed on her arm. She raised her gaze to her daughter's innocent face.

"See, Mama, I told you Santa would bring Daddy home for Christmas."

Although it was a new year, it seemed that the continually falling snow wanted to bury them in the drifts that were still left over from the December snowfall. "I don't think we've had enough of a break to even think about seeing a blade of grass," mused Emma. "Okay, Lord. I know that the prophecy to cleanse the earth by water has been fulfilled and that we are still expecting the day when it will be cleansed by fire, but I don't ever remember reading about the earth being made clean by mounds and mounds of snow . . ."

As Emma headed out the door to tackle the leftovers from last night's storm, she heard the sound of her snow blower being roused from its winter slumber. Since the walks had always been done for her, she'd never needed to start it. But this morning was a different story. Without the blower, the only way to get through the snow was to tunnel through.

"Hey, Paul. Shouldn't you be doing your own walks? I mean, I really, *really* appreciate it," she grinned, "but I do have three strapping sons who can help me with this."

Paul didn't have to hide anymore since Jesse had caught him doing their walks during Christmas break and had grilled him unmercifully about any other "secret" activities. But when the dumbfounded and confused look on Paul's face convinced Jesse that Paul was genuine, Jesse let it go and realized that he was nothing more than just a good friend helping with an overwhelming chore this winter. Their "Santa," Jesse surmised, would probably forever remain (in this life anyway) anonymous.

"What d'ya mean? I got used to getting up so blinkin' early before I got caught, that this is like the middle of the day to me! Besides, without having to stealth around, I can now use this snow hound and make the work go twice as fast." He nodded toward the industrial-sized blower.

Emma smiled and grabbed the shovel so she could clear the residue the blower left behind. Emma invited Paul in for a cup of hot chocolate, but he needed to get home to Marianne. "Give her my love then, and tell her thanks for letting you go out into the harsh cruel world to help widows and orphans alike."

"You know me, just your regular old superhero with extra-skinny legs! See ya, Em." He hugged her before heading back down the now clear driveway.

Emma returned to her living room, where she curled up in her scalloped-edged quilt. She loved Saturdays, especially ones like this where she could curl up and keep warm, count her blessings, and know that wherever William was, he was undoubtedly getting a kick out of her world being covered with a blanket of snow.

Creating a
Santa Letters
Christmas

A Strange Visitor

Original author unknown

Edited by Stacy Gooch-Anderson

Just two nights ago, I had a rather peculiar visit from an even stranger visitor. This is how it happened . . .

I had just finished the household chores and was wrapping up for the night and preparing to go to bed, when I heard a noise coming from the living room. When I went in to check on things, to my surprise Santa Claus himself stepped out from behind the Christmas tree. He placed his fingers over his lips, shushing me so I wouldn't cry out and wake the children slumbering upstairs.

"What are you—" I cut my questioning short when I saw that he had tears in his eyes. His usual jolly manner was gone, leaving behind a shell of the eager, boisterous soul we've all come to know and love.

He answered with a simple statement: "Teach your children." I was puzzled. What did he mean? He anticipated my question and, with one quick movement, brought a red velvet bag from behind the tree.

As I stood there in my pajamas, bewildered, Santa said once again, "Teach your children." My still-perplexed expression must have shown through the near darkness, because he continued on without missing a beat. "Teach them the old meaning of Christmas—the meaning that this world has forgotten."

Santa reached into the toy bag and pulled out a brilliant, shiny star. "Teach the children that the star was the heavenly sign of promise long, long ago. God promised a Savior to the world and a sign that would bear witness to the fulfillment of that promise. That sign was the great star of the east. A star now reminds us of God's love for mankind and his promise fulfilled. When you look to the heavens at night and see a sea of countless stars, remember that they show the burning hope of all mankind."

Santa gently laid the star on the fireplace mantle and then drew from the bag a glittering red ornament.

"Teach your children that red is the first color of Christmas. It was first used by the Lord's faithful people to remind them of the blood that was shed by our Savior. Christ gave his life and his blood that every man might have God's gift to all—eternal life. Red is deep, intense, vivid—it is the greatest color of all the Christmas colors because it symbolizes God and his eldest son's greatest gift to the world."

Santa then reached into his bag and pulled out another

ornament that was a glittering, frosted white. "Teach your children that white is the second color of Christmas. It represents the purity of the Savior—the Lamb of God. Only a perfect man, untainted by the sins and horrors of the world, could offer Himself up as the sacrificial lamb. Christ is the only man who has ever walked the face of the earth who has maintained perfection and purity. And with a clean heart, he laid down a mortal life so he could show us the way to eternity. That selfless act, the purity of his heart, and his life are represented by the second color of Christmas.

As Mr. Claus was twisting and pulling another object out of his bag, I heard the kitchen clock begin its countdown to midnight. I wanted to say something, but Santa, ignoring time, went right on.

"Teach your children," he said as he finally dislodged a small Christmas tree from the depths of the toy bag. He placed it on the floor and gently hung the red and white ornaments and topped it with the star. The deep green was a perfect background for the ornaments. Here was the third color of Christmas.

"The stately fir tree remains green all year round," he said. "This represents the everlasting hope of mankind. Green is the youthful, hopeful, abundant color of nature.

Also notice how all of the tree's needles point heavenward. This is symbolic of how man's thoughts and spirit should always be turned toward heaven. The tree has long since been one of man's best friends. It has sheltered him, warmed him, and made beauty for him. As the tree has done so much for man by enhancing his life, the Savior has given even more by giving him eternal life."

Santa's eyes were once again beginning to twinkle as he stood there. Suddenly I heard a soft tinkling sound, reminding me of a sound from long ago.

"Teach your children that as the lost sheep are found by the sound of the bell, so should its ring remind man to return to God's fold. A bell's sound means guidance for a safe return. It further signifies that all are precious in the eyes of the Lord.

As the surreal sound of the bell faded into the night, Santa then drew out a candle. He placed it on the mantle, letting its tiny flame cast a soft glow about the darkened room. Odd shapes and shadows slowly danced on the walls.

"Teach your children," whispered Santa, "that the candle has multiple meanings. First, it represents the star from long ago. As a candle's small light stands out against the darkness, we remember the star of Bethlehem that illuminated the dark sky, promising hope to a dark world and testifying of the fulfillment of God's promise. At first, candles were placed on Christmas trees to represent the multitude of glowing stars that shine throughout the darkness, but safety has now removed them from the tree and electrical lights have been placed in their stead. Second, and most important, a candle represents our Savior—the light of the world! Just as the flame of such a small candle can illuminate the blackest of spaces, so it is with the Savior, who became the light in a gloomy world as he illuminated men's hearts with hope and life eternal."

Santa snapped his fingers, and instantly hundreds of small white lights illuminated the small tree. He then picked up a gift from under it. He pointed to the large, decorative bow and said, "A bow is placed on a present to remind us of the spirit of brotherhood that should be between men. We need to remember that the bow is tied as men should be tied—all of us together—with the bonds of goodwill. Good will and unity are the messages of the bow."

"Teach your children that the reason we give presents at Christmas is to remind us first of the wise men who sought the Holy babe so they could adore him by placing gifts of value at his feet. Today we adore those we love by giving them gifts at Christmastime. But, even more important, these gifts are to remind us that the Savior himself was God's gift to the world. His adoration for his children came in the form of a Redeemer."

As I began to wonder what else Saint Nick might have in his bag, he surprised me by closing it and slinging it over his shoulder. He then reached up and grabbed a candy cane placed high on our tree. I was caught off guard when he offered it to me.

"Teach your children that the candy cane represents the shepherd's crook. The curved crook on the long staff is used to safely and gently bring back straying sheep. The candy cane represents our Savior's staff and helps us to remember that we should willingly offer aid and a helping hand at Christmastime. The candy cane reminds us that, just as our elder brother keeps careful watch over us, we too should always happily consider ourselves our brothers' keepers."

Santa then paused. He seemed to realize the late hour and that he should be on his way. Soon would be his big day. As he looked about the room, feelings of contentment radiated on his face. My own eyes spoke volumes of wonderment over what I'd learned and the admiration I had for this character who'd shared his Christmas insights with me.

His demeanor was almost back to jovial as he approached the front door. The twinkle in his eye had returned. He wasn't, however, quite through yet. He reached into his bag and brought out a large holly wreath. He placed it upon the door and said, "Please teach your children that the wreath symbolizes the eternal nature of love. It never ends. It is one continuous round of affection. The wreath does double duty while it greets those coming to your door. Not only does it teach of endless love, but it is made of the symbols and all of the colors of Christmas. It reminds us of all the gifts and meanings of Christmas as we celebrate our Savior's holy birth. Please, please teach your children."

I pondered and wondered and thrilled with delight
As I sat and viewed all those symbols at night.
I dozed as I sat in the soft candle's light,
And my thoughts were of Santa and all he'd made right.
To give and to help, to love and to serve,
Are the best things of life that we all deserve.
Old Santa Claus, that jolly plump elf,
Is the very best symbol of Christmas itself.
He's the sign of the gift of love and life,
The ending of evil and ceasing of strife.

His message to me on this Christmas Eve night,
Has opened a treasure of deepest insight.
The one thing on earth we all ought to do,
Is the teaching of children the right and the true.

Santa's Survival Kits for the New Year

Choose a few of the suggestions from below (or be creative and come up with your own) and put them in a sack with a tag attached. Then go wish your friends and neighbors a very Merry Christmas full of love, laughter, and lots of good cheer!

❋ Chocolate hugs and kisses to remind you that you are loved

❋ A tissue or a few squares of toilet paper for those times when you feel "wiped" out

❋ A penlight or matches to help light your way when you're feeling a bit "burned" out

❋ Starlight mints to help you remember that you're worth a "mint"

❋ Taffy or Tootsie Rolls to remind you not to bite off more than you can chew.

❋ A penny to remind you to share your thoughts

❋ Smarties to help you on those days when you don't feel so smart.

❋ Gum so you can easily "chews" your important priorities this season

* Starbursts to give you a burst of energy on those days when you have none

* Any food item (like a packet of soup) to give you food for thought

* Snickers or Laffy Taffy to remind you to take time to laugh

* Raisins to help you remember that you're "raisin' " your cheer meter this year

* A ruler to help you measure your success day by day

* A lightbulb to help you "lighten" your load

* A battery to help you "recharge"

* A candle to remind you to "brighten" someone else's day

* A bag to help you keep it all together

* A packet of Kool-Aid to aid you in keeping your cool when the season overwhelms you

ABOUT THE AUTHOR

Stacy Gooch-Anderson moved often during her growing-up years, living in Phoenix, Anaheim, Chicago, Denver, and St. Louis, and finally ended up in Salt Lake City, where she currently resides with her husband and four sons.

She attended the University of Utah before turning her focus to raising her family. She never abandoned her love of writing, however, and later returned to her roots as a journalist, winning several awards through the Society of Professional Journalists for her feature writing and investigative skills.

She is currently a corporate trainer for new writers and spends her extra time publicly speaking, teaching, and editing a newsletter for her church.

She enjoys reading, learning, anything creative, and soaking in the sunshine with her friends and family.